Saving The Catholic Church While Sitting In A Pew

(Well...Not *Just* Sitting In A Pew!)

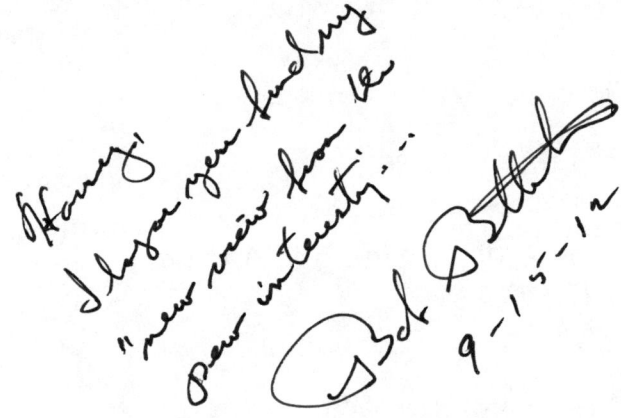

Saving The Catholic Church While Sitting In A Pew

(Well...Not *Just* Sitting In A Pew!)

Robert J. Betterton

2011

Author of
The Compliant, Curious and Critical Catholic (2005)
The Familiar Stranger Who Lives In Our Home (2008)

PRESS

To

The Magnificent Seven:
My Great-Grandchildren,
Adrian Lindsay, Jackson Keating,
Connor Lindsay, Ryan Olivia Keating,
Grayson Keating, "Xander" Lindsay,
Caitlin Carson
And all of their future siblings and cousins.
May you learn to love a Church that is truly
worth saving.

Table of Contents

Here the case is made that both Compliant and Critical Catholics who merely cope with the way the Institutional Church operates are complicit in the troubles it faces. The responsibility for accepting the current situation falls squarely on the people in the pew as does the task of fixing it. After all, Pope John XXIII told us: We are the Church!

There are significant reasons why American Catholics are different from Catholics elsewhere in the world and that might be a clue, not only to the reasons why the problems facing the American Church are what they are, but to disgruntled Catholics in democracies all over the world. Ironically, the American Catholic Church could become a model for the Universal Church.

The history of the doctrine of infallibility is examined as is the phenomenon of "creeping infallibilism", a significant factor among many traditional Catholics, because of their in the lack of knowledge of Church history and the essential difference between matters of Faith and Morals and matters of Governance and Discipline. That ignorance enables actions of the Institutional Church in many areas, detrimental to the Church as a whole.

Myth One among many traditional Catholics is that the Church has operated success-fully in the same way for more than 2,000 years and there is no reason to change that because it is working well. Both premises in that sentence have been incorrect since Vatican I in the 1870's. Vatican II might have helped, but the leadership of Institutional Church since John XXIII has made sure that did not happen.

The perceived conundrum of the Holy Spirit arises when one wonders how the Holy Spirit could let the Catholic Church get into the serious trouble in which it finds itself. In this chapter we ask the question: If you have Infallibility, who needs the Holy Spirit? The answer is: We all do, especially those who allow claims of Infallibility by extension.

One statement on which you can appar-ently find a high degree of agreement between traditional Catholics and progres-sive Catholics is that Vatican II is the main source of the problems of today. Those who are traditional say it went too far. Those who are progressive say it didn't go far enough. They are both wrong. Vatican II was eviscerated by the machinations of the Institutional Church.

The least likely cause of the defections from Catholicism and the problems created by the Institutional Church, is Vatican II. The problems were not created by those who left, but by those who stayed. They sat quietly in the pews (where there is now much more room) and let things happen the way they have. No one among us has stood up and said loudly, "Stop! This is not the way!" In other words, no one answered the famous question "What would Jesus Do" correctly. As Pogo said, "We has met the enemy and they is us".

Here are the views of two prominent Catholics, on a Bishop in Australia, the other a noted author and Vatican expert on the aftermath of Vatican II. They describe the careful transformation of John Paul II at the hands of then Cardinal Ratzinger; their subsequent joint dismantling of the successes of Vatican II and the efforts of their Institutional Church to take us back to the nineteenth century.

Governance is the way the Institutional Church operates and does its business in accordance with its own man-made rules. In this chapter we will discuss issues like Celibacy, Bishops, the Roman Curia, Collegiality, Canon Law, Clerical Sex Abuse, Magisterium and Autochthony.

There are so many issues of Discipline that it was necessary to cover them in two chapters rather than one. This one deals with things

Acknowledgements

The basic inspiration for this book came from a long-running conversation indulged in a series of once-a-month or so dinners over a period of five to six years with my good friend and fellow critical Catholic Ron Naumann, concerning the Catholic Church. When I began to put those ideas and situations on paper Ron assumed the role of a critical reader, which is impossible to define except that he made me think and allowed me to ignore his suggestions. I have known Dr. Naumann for fifty-nine years.

I had two other such readers, Barbara Geary Reynolds and Ann Cassidy Stiner, both of whom I believe have known me longer than almost anyone on the planet, although I have not seen Barbara in person for about sixty-eight years.

Barbara taught Religious Studies for twenty-two years at the high school level in three schools in the Metropolitan New York area. For the last seven of those years she was Chair of the Religious Studies Department at Fordham Prep in the Bronx. Barbara also clearly qualifies as a critical Catholic.

Ann was also a teacher at the Elementary level of CCD. She is closer to being a Compliant Catholic than the other three of us, but admits that reading this book has made her much more curious about things pertaining to the Institutional Church.

I quoted a large number of sources in this book, I believe all with attribution. However, I have never been very good at footnotes, so I hope I can address them here. They were: Rev. Richard P. McBrien, from his book *The Church: The Evolution of Catholicism*, HarperOne 2008; Rev. John W. O'Malley SJ, from *What Happened at Vatican II*, Harvard Press, 2008; Rev. Francis X. Murphy CSsR, aka Xavier Rynne from *Vatican Council II*, Orbis Books 1999; Robert Blair Kaiser, from *A Church In Search of Itself: Benedict XVI and the Battle for the Future*, Vintage Books 2007 and *Cardinal Mahony: A Novel*, Sue Knopf 2007.

There are a few quotations from articles by Father Charles E. Curran, a fellow Rochesterian, who I have never met but have been in his audience; several named and unnamed spokespersons from the USCCB; and others.

The New Advent Catholic Encyclopedia online, (http://www.newadvent.org/cathen/) was also quoted frequently.

With regard to speeches by prominent Catholics, I quoted extensively from Mr. Kaiser's speech at the Humbert Summer School in Ireland on August 19, 2010, entitled "Catholic Church Reform: No More Thrones".

I also quoted the entire talk, "The Need For Servant Leadership In The Catholic Church" by Bishop Kevin Dowling of Rustenburg, South Africa addressing a group in Cape Town given on June 1, 2010 about the Restoration movement by the Vatican.

Finally, I had great difficulty in clearly stating the distinction between references to "Church" meaning *all of its members*, laity and clerical as Pope Blessed John XXIII taught us at the outset of Vatican II, and "Church" in the form of an administrative organization, in which its hierarchy manages though rules of governance and discipline.

To resolve this, at the suggestion of Barbara Reynolds I adopted the term Institutional Church for the latter. This was used much earlier, but in the same context by Cardinal Avery Dulles, SJ in his book *Models of the Church*, Doubleday 1974. In it one of the models he discusses is that of the Institutional Church.

I have appropriated the term and when I use it, I am referring to the Church hierarchy including the Pope, the Roman Curia and all Bishops, particularly in matters of the Governance and Discipline in the Roman Catholic Church. I do not discuss matters of Faith and Morals in this book, frankly because I generally have little discomfort with them.

Introduction

When I was writing my first book *The Compliant, Curious and Critical Catholic*, I asked my good friend, Father Bill O'Malley SJ how I would know when I was finished. He has written about thirty-five books and knows all the answers to questions like that. His reply was, "The book will tell you".

So I kept on writing and found that he was correct. One day I knew it was finished. Just like that. It wasn't that I didn't have more to say, just that I didn't need to say it there.

This book is different. It told me when it was *starting*. Unfortunately, it didn't do that until I had already written several pretty interesting chapters. I ended up tossing them out because they clearly did not belong in the book I was beginning to write, whether I wanted them to or not.

Since *The C, C & C Catholic* has been published many who read it have asked if I were going to write more about my personal relationship with the Catholic Church. My usual answer was "been there, done that and have a few royalties to prove it". When one writes his first book at the age of seventy-five and feels that he has some things to say on other subjects, it might be better to not spend one's remaining years writing about the same thing more than once.

Besides, that first book was about as militant as I was comfortable with and since it obviously didn't cause a great revolution I must admit that it was becoming more difficult to maintain even that level of militancy. I guess maybe you become that way when you approach eighty.

However, the questions about another book continued and I began to try to think of an interesting approach for it. After a while, I found one with which I thought I could have some fun.

This book began as *The Coping Catholic,* a hopefully humorous, definitely tongue-in-cheek diary of an aging Critical Catholic, who is still at the same time doggedly faithful to his beliefs and intellectually militant, but weary of the intransigent, arrogant, self-serving posturing of the Institutional Church.

At first it moved along pretty well, but after a several thousand words and three of four chapters I decided that I needed to clearly define the "State of the Church" in order to set up the funny stuff. I was confident that I could state the vagaries of the Institutional Church in such a way as to make the humor work. However, that frame of mind did not last long.

As I tried to describe the issues I see facing the Church, I began to become angrier and angrier. For a person of Faith, who loves his Church, this is not the stuff of humor and was definitely not a time for coping. There are plenty of issues to inspire both criticism and militancy. Today is the time to be militant in whatever way one can, to save our Church from itself.

This is not a book on Faith and Morals or Revelation and Tradition. It is about the arcane, unjust, arbitrary and discriminatory man-made rules of Governance and Discipline designed and implemented by the Institutional Church to maintain its power and control over the Faithful. These are issues that affect us every day.

Fortunately for me as an author, though unfortunately for me as a practicing Catholic, the Church provides an endless stream of actions and inactions, which should make any educated and intelligent Catholic critical of his or her Church. However, that raised other issues I had to face.

Many Catholics *are* educated *and* intelligent. However, probably because the Institutional Church wants it that way, they generally *are not intellectually curious* about the origins of the problems or the reasons for the positions of the Institutional Church on them. As a result they are painfully unaware of the truth and how they have been systematically misled.

In order to get my message across I had to make them convinced of this situation. At the same time I realized that for some reason many Catholics are so defensive about the Institutional Church that they *do not want* to hear the truth. The word brainwashed comes readily to mind.

These people have developed an "us and them" mentality regarding *anyone* who dares to be critical of the Institutional Church. If the book were to have a chance of convincing anyone, I would have to develop a "we and others of us" mindset in my audience.

I decided to make all my arguments "within the family". The only people with a voice in the debate in *this* book would be practicing Catholics in good standing. People who have left the Church, regardless of how relevant their experiences and opinions might be would not be quoted in these pages. I needed to demonstrate *that people other than me* can be *Catholic and critical* of the Institutional Church at the same time.

In this effort, my first discovery was how much valuable information supporting my positions on issues was available from *Catholic* sources, including the *Catholic Encyclopedia* and documents from Vatican II, as well as articles, speeches and books by well known Catholic scholars and authors. All of the supporting information in this book comes from such sources. My plan was to use Catholics to convince other Catholics. I found many who have been trying to do just that.

There are a number of organizations of Catholics who have left the Church. Most of them are special interest groups, usually devoted to single issues such as celibacy, women priests and birth control. They often have powerful arguments and points of view. However, in order to avoid being tarred with the same brush as they I have elected to not include any of them here.

My second discovery and by far the more important came when I began to discuss some critical issues with traditional Catholics who I had always considered to be very knowledgeable about their faith. The discovery was that they had very little knowledge about the history of the Church and the details of the evolution of its policies of Governance and Discipline. That is not because the information is not there. It is because either they are just uninterested in anything that disturbs their abiding belief in the status quo, or they are too lazy to look for it.

I had to waken that interest in average Catholics. I had to start fires in their bellies. I had to make them angry, not at me, but at how far our Church is from where it could and should be.

I am sure that some of you *will* become angry at me and be tempted to dismiss me as some kind of a misanthrope with an axe to grind. If that should happen, I am going to suggest something that I suspect few other authors would.

If I really get you angry with me, stop reading and turn to the last chapter in the book. Read it, swallow hard and then go back to where you were and finish the book. I think it may change your thinking about some things.

Chapter One

Catholics Who Cope

On a chilly autumn afternoon in the late Fifties, a woman walked briskly down a street in an unfamiliar Brooklyn neighborhood. She had taken a New York Central train down from Albany earlier in the day and then a subway to the stop written on the piece of paper in her hand, which also included the street address of her destination. When she passed a meticulously cared for, but rather crowded parish cemetery she knew she was nearly there.

The woman paused for a moment in front of a small, neat rectory to gather her thoughts, then went up the steps and rang the bell. A housekeeper arrived quickly and after learning the nature of the woman's visit, ushered her into a pleasant sitting room.

The Pastor, replete in his cassock, entered and greeted her warmly. After a few pleasantries the woman told him that her husband had recently died. She said that on his death bed he told her that he wanted to be buried in the cemetery of the Brooklyn parish in which he had grown up.

The good father expressed his condolences and said that although their little cemetery was nearly full, they gave priority to anyone who had been baptized in that parish. He checked a dusty ledger to confirm that was the case and said he would make all the arrangements. Then he asked where the deceased's remains were located.

The woman opened her oversized pocketbook, took out a large, plain jar and placed it on the table between them. The Pastor nearly had apoplexy and quickly showed the woman the door, assuring her that if she should somehow reach heaven, it would be fruitless to look around for her husband.

Shaken, the woman started her return home, but as she passed the cemetery again, she noticed there was a bench that she had not seen before. She sat down and had a good cry.

When she arrived home in Albany, she called her late husband's brother Ed in Syracuse and told him what had happened. Ed asked her what she did then.

She told him that by the time she stopped crying it was beginning to get dark and the lights had come on in a hardware store across the street. She went over to the store and bought a small hand trowel. When she returned to the cemetery it was almost completely dark as she carried out her intended mission.

"He's in there and they don't even know it", she proudly proclaimed.

Ed was a close friend of my father and he told him the story. When Dad told me, it was the first time I had ever heard of a Coping Catholic.

Coping is a very good word and an even better concept. It means handling or dealing with an issue or a situation without compromising one's often strong beliefs. That is important. It does not mean accepting defeat. One must never confuse coping with acquiescence, which is to be avoided by people of principle at all cost. It also means dissenting by one's very presence.

In an earlier book I defined modern American Catholics into three categories: those who are Compliant with virtually every aspect of Catholicism through total, unquestioning acceptance of everything that is taught (even though that often includes conjecture on the part of other laymen whose opinion they respect); those who are pro-actively Curious, searching independently for verification or at least clarification of Church teaching on subjects with which they have some level of doubt; and finally, those who have become informed enough by that Curiosity to become legitimately Critical and able to defend those positions.

For me and many like me, those were also personal stages through which I passed in my now eighty year relationship with the Catholic Church.

We Critical Catholics are often misunderstood. Most of us are not calling for an ecclesiastical revolution, but merely some long overdue modifications and reform of man-made policies. You know, just like the aggiornamento promised by John XXIII, embraced by the Second Vatican Council but systematically dismantled by John's successors.

By definition, there is a great deal about our Faith, with which we have absolutely no disagreement. For example, I personally have no difficulty at all regarding any of the precepts included in the basic enumerations of Church dogma, the Apostles Creed and the Nicene Creed. They are beliefs for which I hope I would have had the courage to take on the lions.

When it comes to dogma, the position of most Curious and Critical Catholics is usually not rejection, but what we consider to be legitimate doubt. For us, that legitimate doubt is not a deal breaker and, instead of getting all worked up about it we tend to just ignore the dogma. These are often concepts which rarely if ever affect us directly. We just shake our heads and move on.

A good example of this indifference is my long held attitude about Original Sin. I understood that Adam and Eve (or whatever the names were of those ancestors of ours who first were given souls) sinned against God (for whatever it was that they did) and deserved to be punished. However, I couldn't figure out what that really had to do with me. I didn't understand why the Nuns said that I had a "stain" on my soul from the moment of my birth (or was that the moment of my implantation on the uterine wall, or the moment of the fertilization of an embryo).

It seemed strange that a just God would do that to everyone just because the first people screwed up and besides, if He did do that to everyone didn't it just become part of our standard equipment to be dealt with like freckles or red hair? Why was that a big deal?

However, those same Nuns told me that Baptism washed that stain away. Since it was seven or eight years after the fact when they told me about this, I rarely think about it and certainly don't worry at all.

I did have some questions about non-Catholic friends of mine who had not been baptized. Then I realized that probably no one told them about the stains, so why should I bring it up and make them worry. Then I guess I decided that God probably only put the stain on Catholic souls because they had a way to get rid of it. That seemed logical at the time. Or at least it was as logical as the stain being there.

Ironically, when I was writing these last two paragraphs, my curiosity took over and I wondered what the Catholic Encyclopedia had to say about Original Sin, those stains and my perception of injustice. So I looked it up.

I have found that one attribute of the Catholic Encyclopedia is that it tends to tell you much more than you really want to know, but after all the discussion of how the doctrine evolved I found two very clear paragraphs:

"...according to Catholic theology man has not lost his natural faculties: by the sin of Adam he has been deprived only of the Divine gifts to which his nature had no strict right, the complete mastery of his passions, exemption from death, sanctifying grace, the vision of God in the next life. The Creator, whose gifts were not due to the human race, had the right to bestow them on such conditions as He wished and to make their conservation depend on... fidelity..."

And:

"...The absence of sanctifying grace in the new-born child is also an effect of the first sin, for Adam, having received holiness and justice from God, lost it not only for himself but also for us...If he has lost it for us we were to have received it from him at our birth with the other prerogatives of our race. Therefore the absence of sanctifying grace in a child is a real privation; it is the want of something that should have been in him according to the Divine plan. If this favor is not merely something physical but is something in the moral order, if it is holiness, its privation may be called a sin. But sanctifying grace is holiness and is so called by the Council of Trent, because holiness consists in union with God, and grace unites us intimately with God. Moral goodness consists in this, that our action is according to the moral law, but grace is deification as the Fathers say, a perfect conformity with God who is the first rule of all morality... Sanctifying grace therefore enters into the moral order, not as an act that passes but as a permanent tendency which exists even when the subject who possesses it does not act; it is a turning towards God, *conversio ad Deum*. Consequently the privation of this grace, even without any other act, would be a stain, a moral deformity, a turning away from God, *aversio a Deo*, and this character is not found in any other effect of the fault of Adam. This privation, therefore, is the hereditary stain."

Well, why the hell didn't they say so, in the first place! Other than the terribly judgmental misuse of the words "hereditary stain on the soul" of a new-born, I can believe that and happily it provides a perfect segue to two other examples, one a doctrine with which I have no problem, the Immaculate Conception and the other one about which I am not quite so sure, the Assumption. I believe that I can explain that apparent inconsistency.

Now, of course I must first explain (mostly for the benefit of Compliant Catholics) about the Immaculate Conception. Contrary to popular belief among many Catholics, the Immaculate Conception has nothing to do with the virgin birth. It deals with *Mary's* conception. The misconception (I couldn't resist that) probably flows from a general impression that the Church welcomes if not fosters, the notion that sexual activity is somewhat of an unclean necessity.

It makes perfect sense to me that for a woman to carry and deliver the Son of God, she must have first possessed holiness at the level we describe as Sanctifying Grace. Since I believe that God is capable of anything *that must be done,* it makes sense that He infused that grace in her and what other time makes more sense than at her conception. In that context, it seems to me to be an unnecessary and irrelevant rationale that it had to be done that way to avoid Original Sin.

I consider the Assumption to be a totally different case. Although God could certainly have made it happen, there was no imperative for it. In the larger context, it doesn't matter one way or the other whether it happened or not and God certainly didn't need to impress anyone. Why would God waste His time doing it if it doesn't matter, especially since no one witnessed it and recorded it at the time? And if it really happened, why wouldn't that be mentioned somewhere in The Acts of the Apostles?

Perhaps this is merely an effort to get the Apostles off the hook for not paying proper attention to the fate and disposition of the remains of the mother of Jesus. It may just be the work of well-meaning early apologists.

The actual need for the existence of the *doctrine* is simple. No one knew where Mary's remains were buried or whether she was cremated to avoid desecration for that matter. So a doctrine was developed to explain it. The underlying rationale most people give is that God did not want his earthly mother buried in the dirt and I suppose that is understandable. Yet that is what usually happens to us earthly people. What about "Remember man that thou art dust and unto dust thou shall return"? That seems like a slippery slope argument headed for a Blessed Quartet to me.

Here is what the Catholic Encyclopedia says about the facts of the Assumption. I have included the entire quotation because it is all that anyone really knows about the subject:

"Regarding the day, year, and manner of Our Lady's death, nothing certain is known. Catholic faith, however, has always derived our knowledge of the mystery from Apostolic Tradition. Epiphanius (d. 403) acknowledged that he knew nothing definite about it (Haer., lxxix, 11). The dates assigned for it vary between three and fifteen years after Christ's Ascension. Two cities claim to be the place of her departure: Jerusalem and Ephesus. Common consent favors Jerusalem, where her tomb is shown; but some argue in favor of Ephesus. The first six centuries did not know of the tomb of Mary at Jerusalem.

The belief in the corporeal assumption of Mary is founded on the apocryphal treatise *De Obitu S. Dominae*, bearing the name of St. John, which belongs however to the fourth or fifth century. It is also found in the book *De Transitu Virginis*, falsely ascribed to St. Melito of Sardis, and in a spurious letter attributed to St. Denis the Areopagite. If we consult genuine writings in the East, it is mentioned in the sermons of St. Andrew of Crete, St. John Damascene, St. Modestus of Jerusalem and others. In the West, St. Gregory of Tours (De gloria mart., I, iv) mentions it first. The sermons of St. Jerome and St. Augustine for this feast, however, are spurious. St. John of Damascus (P.G., I, 96) thus formulates the tradition of the Church of Jerusalem:

St. Juvenal, Bishop of Jerusalem, at the Council of Chalcedon (451), made known to the Emperor Marcian and Pulcheria, who wished to possess the body of the Mother of God, that Mary died in the presence of all the Apostles, but that her tomb, when opened, upon the request of St. Thomas, was found empty; wherefrom the Apostles concluded that the body was taken up to heaven.

Today, the belief in the corporeal assumption of Mary is universal in the East and in the West; according to Benedict XIV (De Festis B.V.M., I, viii, 18) it is a probable opinion, which to deny were impious and blasphemous."

Despite the lack of any demonstrable facts, also from the Catholic Encyclopedia is this:

"By promulgating the Bull Munificentissimus Deus, 1 November, 1950, Pope Pius XII declared infallibly that the Assumption of the Blessed Virgin Mary was a dogma of the Catholic Faith. Likewise, the Second Vatican Council taught in the Dogmatic Constitution Lumen Gentium that "the Immaculate Virgin, preserved free from all stain of original sin, was taken up body and soul into heavenly glory, when her earthly life was over, and exalted by the Lord as Queen over all things."

This is not an abstract interpretation of a Theological principle. It is a conclusion drawn from fancy rather than fact. Consider again the following from the Catholic Encyclopedia account:

- It states clearly and without reservation that "Regarding the day, year, and manner of Our Lady's death, nothing certain is known."
- Anyone living after 403 AD can hardly be considered an Apostle, which seems to eliminate the Apostolic Tradition argument.
- The underlying belief is based on and "apocryphal treatise" of unknown provenance four to five hundred years after the fact; a book that was apparently plagiarized; a spurious letter with no attribution; and finally an excuse to an Emperor,

who wanted "to possess the body of the Mother of God" that "Mary died in the presence of all the Apostles, but that her tomb, when opened, upon the request of St. Thomas, was found empty; wherefrom the Apostles concluded that the body was taken up to heaven." Yet none of this is mentioned in either the Gospels as a significant event after the Resurrection, like that other demonstration of the doubt of Thomas (was Thomas really merely a metaphor for rational, human doubt?) or the certainly less important incident on the road to Emmaus, or in the Acts of the Apostles.

- Finally the statement that "according to Benedict XIV (De Festis B.V.M., I, viii, 18) it is a probable opinion, which to deny were impious and blasphemous" raises the question of the credibility of a "probable opinion" and is certainly not a ringing endorsement.

Does that mean that I reject the doctrine of the Assumption as untrue? Absolutely not. I believe that God is capable of *anything that must be done*, but I find no imperative that the Assumption *had to have happened*. I find nothing to convince me it did. I may be wrong. Moreover, it is another irrelevance that Catholics are forced to defend in dealing with people of less Faith.

I do have some questions with what I consider the trivia of faith. I don't understand what angels are really about, although I don't ever lose any sleep over them and I am rather uncomfortable with the characterization of God or Christ as an earthly-like king. I also think that hell is reserved for those who are really the worst of the worst and it is not significantly populated.

I question the value of some kinds of petitionery prayer, probably because I grew up praying after every Mass and whenever else it could be inserted, for the conversion of Russia. All those Catholics saying all those prayers for all those years and we know how well that turned out.

I said that one day recently to a Compliant Catholic friend and he claimed that those prayers were all answered when the Berlin Wall came down. Of course, he gave equal credit to Ronald Reagan. I was going to point out that it was Russia we were praying for, not Germany and "Besides, it was the economy, stupid", but I knew he wouldn't get it. And does it really matter?

Then there are the arcane practices that I question like the nine First Fridays to assure a happy death (since you can only have one happy death, why should you do them more than once?); novenas that "never fail"; and claims that apparently paranormal occurrences are all miracles.

I don't understand why certain prayers only work when said a prescribed number of times or at a specific time, but regardless of the time zone you are in. Then there is the idea that someone among us is qualified to establish the criteria for sainthood, much less measure anyone against it.

Most of the things about which I have doubt, though not total disbelief, are those doctrines promulgated long after the fact by zealous but ill-informed Councils or Popes in reaction to some passing crisis of belief. I feel that in some cases expediency has trumped logic and reason.

My real criticism is centered on the governance, management, administration and operational style of the Institutional Church and I feel that these issues must be quickly addressed or the future of the Church is bleak. These are not really issues of Faith although they are frequently referred to as such by those whose "faith" is really more monolithic than monotheistic.

In retrospect I think that after my earlier book came out, I made a mistake by calling myself a "Critical Catholic" rather than a Catholic who is critical about some things. That makes it just too easy for traditional Catholics as well as former Catholics to put down one's position.

In fact, some have said things like, "If you find the Church hierarchy so lacking; if you find so many rules and regulations onerous; if you find so many of its beliefs archaic; if you find so many of its dogmas so unreasonable; why do you not just leave?"

The answer is that I am simply a traditional practicing Catholic who, in the Jesuit educational tradition of critical thinking has made the effort to become informed on issues, considered the facts carefully and developed reasoned critical positions about certain teachings and practices of the Institutional Church. In other words, we Critical Catholics are thinking and reasonable people who are happy to engage in debate, but will not be bullied, no matter from whose pulpit.

Our rationale is the belief that people, regardless of their best intentions can be mistaken either on the issue itself or in its application. It is reasonable for us to disagree until convinced through logic and at least some evidence. This is simply a proper use of the free will, which defines our humanity. It is also the belief that in God's plan for us, some things just don't matter very much.

I have both consciously and conscientiously done that rather than just leaving. That begs the question: If *I* can accept the intransigence of the Institutional Church and its Compliant members, why can't those who are dismissive of people like me merely because *they* can't handle it, accept my curiosity and criticism?

Before going any further, I must say that from time to time and more frequently than I would like, people say, "Okay, I understand, you are just one of those Liberal Catholics". I am pleased that they understand my position, but I personally have no idea what a Liberal Catholic is or what makes them so. It sounds like a made-up concept or some kind of an artificial oxymoron.

It would seem to have more to do with *ideology* than Theology and I am really not into ideology, because ideology implies an agenda broad enough to attract a following and to really be a follower one must embrace the entire agenda.

When I have asked what those people mean by Liberal Catholic, they get rather vague about it and say things like "You know, you want to change everything" or "You know, you only believe what you like" or the classic, "You know what I mean and don't tell me you don't".

How can I know what you mean, if you will not tell me? I certainly don't want to change everything and I don't know what I would change everything to, if I did.

Lord knows, I don't just believe what I *like*. Who would *like* to believe in the possibility of eternal damnation? Who would *like* to believe that his or her life had no purpose other than self-gratification? Who would *like* to have to constantly defend things with which they don't agree?

The more I have thought about this Liberal Catholic thing, the more I realized that it is merely an extension of the Liberal – Conservative political metaphor that is often, incidentally, used by the same people. Many if not all Compliant Catholics are absolutely "change averse" as are most Conservative politicians. In the minds of Compliant Catholics, *any* change is heresy and acceptance of such change is apostasy, regardless of what the change was. Even if it was good!

I became aware of this feeling to some degree when I wrote my first book. Since I was born, raised and lived the first thirty-three years of my life in Syracuse, New York I have a great many Catholic relatives, friends and acquaintances there. When I was living in the Syracuse Diocese, I pretty much thought it was like any other Diocese.

I particularly assumed that it was much like the Rochester Diocese, which it bordered. After all, why shouldn't I? The Minor and Major Seminaries for the Syracuse Diocese were at that time operated by and located in the Rochester Diocese. The only Bishop of Syracuse I had known was a native of Rochester and he had confirmed me and presented me both my high school diploma and my college Bachelor's degree.

It was only after my book was published that I discovered that many Catholics in Syracuse considered the Diocese of Rochester to be "extremely liberal" and therefore somehow that explained for them the way I think about things. There were comments like: "Well, Rochester has always been more liberal than Syracuse" and "It is obvious where you live now".

I think I was most offended by the implication that my personal position on issues could be so easily influenced by where I lived or the people with whom I associate. What does that say about their opinion of my integrity?

Ironically, we moved to the Rochester area in 1964, while Vatican II was in progress. I became aware that Bishop Walter A. Foery of Syracuse had attended the first session of the Council in 1962, left in disgust with the way he thought things were headed and never returned. I learned that because in Rochester I often played golf with another Walter A. Foery at the club to which we both belonged. He was the Bishop's nephew and a staunch Catholic, but he always seemed a bit amused at his uncle's intransigence, particularly about things that really made sense to him.

The more I have thought about these seemingly unrelated things, the more I realized that the two immediately adjacent Dioceses of Rochester and Syracuse are a metaphor for the condition of the Church today. Depending on one's point of view or in some cases merely one's address the problem is reduced to an unfounded belief either that the Diocese of Rochester is too liberal or that the Diocese of Syracuse is too reactionary, rather than whether it is right or wrong.

Actually, the Diocese of Rochester embraced Papal proclamations of Vatican II findings far more quickly than did the Diocese of Syracuse. Since each of those findings was agreed to by more than 70% of the world's Bishops and duly promulgated by the Pope, it would appear that the Diocese of Rochester operated in the more conservative manner. It would seem the Diocese of Syracuse was the entity of non-conformance or perhaps defiance, though not due to liberalism as usually defined, but more like libertarianism. At the very least they were guilty of dissent.

We will get to Vatican II in a later chapter, but in his book *What Happened at Vatican II* author John W. O'Malley, SJ never refers to opposing sides in the debates as liberal and conservative, but rather as the majority and the minority. That is partially an acknowledgement that the make-up of the two sides was not always the same, but it is also an indication that the opponents were those who considered the status quo to be inviolate and those who did not, rather than dealing with the issues themselves.

The term Critical evokes assumptions of at least some degree of militancy beyond mere debate, however over time militancy reaches the point of diminishing returns and continued debate or coping are all that is left. One can continue to be true to one's critical beliefs and support the militants, but beyond that, some choose to merely cope. It is like resigning one's self to living out one's life as a member of a minority political party.

As a practical matter, I suspect that the current generation, that is those now in their twenties and thirties will not produce many Critical Catholics who stay around. It is too easy for this instant gratification group to just press the re-set button and walk away.

Therefore the number of coping Critical Catholics will decline rapidly and virtually disappear over the next forty years. That is a shame, because the Church needs the coping Critical Catholics in order to maintain its vitality. However, even coping requires dedication and commitment.

Ironically, I believe one could also argue that Coping is the fourth stage in the evolution of a Catholic and perhaps its final stage because it is a complete affirmation of the Critical Catholic's basic Faith. It is even a form of militancy in that it is an assertion that one can be a practicing Catholic despite those elements of the Church of which one is strongly critical.

Coping is sort of a "Don't tell *me* I can't be both Critical *and* Catholic" statement.

The fact is that when people say such things it appears that they don't really understand that a Critical Catholic is interested in reform, not abandonment... besides, as Peter said, "Lord, to whom could we go?" (John 6:68)

These Catholics do not cease to be Critical; in fact they often become even more critical because freed from the need to be militant about *their* key issues they often realize that there are more and more things about which to be critical. In some ways, one might say they *are* somewhat like Compliant Catholics, but with their intellectual curiosity and Free Will intact.

Our Institutional Church, as distinguished from the Church John XXIII told us that *we* were seems to have an infinite capacity for making judgments or taking positions or doing things, which lend themselves to criticism or at the very least questions that deserve answers, which are rarely forthcoming. Sadly, this often seems to flow from arrogance, making it even worse. However, that Curiosity thing kicks in and when the reasoning doesn't add up, it results in Criticism, if not militancy.

Except for the fact that I am writing this book, which is really an act of militancy, I am now a Coping Catholic and when it is published, I may revert to that role...I think...or perhaps not.

That said, coping or militant, being a Catholic is a major part of who, and what I am.

Recently, I attended the funeral of an old friend. It was in an old Episcopal church in a neighborhood once inhabited by the wealthy of Rochester, NY. When I entered, I felt a definite culture shock.

The interior was in the dark, gothic style of Catholic churches in the first half of the last century. It had an old style, elevated pulpit, a communion rail and on the altar there was veil over the chalice folded in that peculiar, yet so familiar fashion.

The service followed the pattern of a Catholic Mass and the prayers from the English Book of Common Prayer were almost identical to those I hear and say each week in my home church, three or four miles away. The Episcopal Priest donned the traditional vestments before the Mass began. I admit that I tried to see if he was wearing a maniple, but I could not be sure.

At the outset of the Mass, the Priest invited all to receive communion. I decided that out of respect for my friend, I would do that.

During the "consecration" I listened very carefully to the identical, familiar words of the Priest, but when they were uttered I had this strange feeling that nothing happened up there at the altar. The words were the same and spoken reverently, but I sensed that "they just didn't work". I could not get over that feeling.

Many of my Catholic friends who were there went to communion. I did not have any problem with that, but I stayed in my seat not feeling that I was missing a thing.

After the service, I ran into and old friend and fellow parishioner as I was going out the door. He is several years older than I, a daily communicant, probably less

Critical, but certainly still Curious. In his usual gruff and direct way he said, "Nice service. Kind of reminded me of the old days...I noticed that several of 'us' went to communion...I was going to, out of respect...but after the consecration I thought, why bother".

I learned a great deal about the depth of my Faith and his that morning.

I cannot conceive of attending Mass and not participating in the Eucharist. I also cannot conceive of, when the Eucharistic Minister says "This is the body of Christ" or "This is the blood of Christ" not responding in my usual firm and unequivocal voice, "AMEN!" However, that does not mean that I cannot be critical of some of the practices and dogmas of the Institutional Church.

I can sit there in the pew and wonder why the homilist did not have the courage to comment on the health care debate in any way and allowed to stand the US Conference of Catholic Bishops' outrageously ignorant pronouncement that the plan should be defeated because they wanted additional assurances that funds cannot be used for abortion, when the Hyde Amendment, which is the law of the land already does that. That was itself an attack on *living* babies and their parents.

I can also wonder why the contrary opinions of the nuns in this debate were discounted and ignored, when they are the people "in the trenches" working with those who need help, rather than just following the Vatican line in an unwinnable debate. The Church lost the legality of abortion debate long ago. It is time to strongly and unequivocally condemn the sin and move on.

I can wonder why there is no mention of the Pope's invitation to the Anglicans to join us, when that includes married priests and all, however our current priests must remain celibate. And male. Does the homilist not care, or is he intimidated, or jealous.

I can wonder how Pope Pius XII can be considered for sainthood when, while knowing that the Holocaust was underway he remained silent and did nothing to stop it, even though he was probably the only one who might have been successful in doing that.

I can wonder why they can't see that conferring sainthood in this case is a mockery of Christian values and calls the very concept of sainthood into question. How does the Institutional Church get off deciding who is a saint anyway? Shouldn't we, the Church be consulted?

I can wonder why a parish, which weekend in and weekend out draws nearly 2,000 people to Mass has not produced a single, home grown parish priest in the nearly fifty years I have been a member and, according to its published history has not in its entire hundred year existence.

I can wonder how the Bishop can announce a $5,490,000 goal for the 2009 annual Diocesan Appeal of and assign quotas to each parish (ours $192,044) without any specific detail as to how it will be used, how success is to be measured or any discussion of whether that is even a good idea. And I definitely don't understand why the Bishop can't let that appeal stand on its own and not require that the parishes guarantee its results. That is not a Diocesan Appeal. It is a Diocesan Tax and clearly taxation without representation.

I can wonder about why the absurdity of the Pope saying that if he gave in and allowed the use of condoms in Africa to stop the spread of AIDS that it would actually increase the danger, is not challenged by any priest with a brain in his head, much less a soul. Of course he did make an exception for male prostitutes; before he didn't.

I can also wonder aloud about these things and others with my friends of nearly fifty years as we walk out of the Church, confident that it is still _our_ Church, despite its many flaws.

I attend and participate in the Mass because I am a Catholic and that is far more important to me than any Priest, Bishop, Cardinal, Pope or any other issue. I can do that and feel comfortable about being critical because in that I celebrate God's greatest gift to us, our Free Will.

In other words, I can cope but I don't have to be happy about what is happening to my Church.

Actually, coping is really pretty easy in many parishes. Rarely does a homilist deliver anything, with which most people cannot generally agree...if they listen.

How can that be? Christ was clearly a radical. When and why did His Church lose that spirit?

I am not sure whether the homilists have just as much difficulty with the troublesome issues as the Critical Catholic, or they don't have the will and the courage to confront them, or they have been instructed by the Bishop to not rock the boat. In any case, that in itself is troubling or at least evidence of trouble.

Occasionally, we have a Baptism during Mass. Although I sometimes find that distracting, the ceremony includes a recitation of the Creed, which I accept without compromise and I feel justified when the Priest says without equivocation, *"This* then, is our Faith". I accept that and believe everything else is negotiable. After all, why would a Priest knowingly mislead a baby?

I go to Mass to celebrate that Faith, despite the problems I have with the institution, which sometimes presents it so clumsily.

I began writing *The Compliant, Curious And Critical Catholic* in 2003 and published it in the fall of 2005. In it I discussed some of the issues I have with the Catholic Church, which I thought would resonate with the largest number of people. Most were issues of policy and practice, which was part of my thesis that it is the Institutional Church and particularly its hierarchy that gets between the practicing Catholic and his or her Faith. I talked about the promise of Vatican II and the betrayal of that promise by the Vatican bureaucracy.

Ironically, just before I sent the manuscript to the publisher, Pope John Paul II died and Benedict XVI was elected his successor. I delayed submission of the manuscript while I added another chapter in which I suggested some things I thought this new Pope might do to halt the Church's plunge to irrelevance. However, I held little hope that he would do that, or for that matter that he would even want to.

I do not claim any gift of prescience in the matter, because as you will learn later, there were few around who thought that our current Holy Father had either the vision or the will to take the correct path. There is no joy in the knowledge that we were absolutely correct.

There is considerable consensus, at least among Critical Catholics regarding this Pope and how he has defined his mission. That consensus is that the Pope believes that his primary mission is to defend the Church against *any* change and in fact to roll things back to the point we were well prior to Vatican II, but not before Vatican I because he treasures that concept of primacy and its corollary infallibility. I believe that consensus is correct. It is about him. That saddens me deeply.

Why would anyone in the Pope's position, want to risk that the Church might not survive the first half of the twenty-first century? Why would he not welcome the opportunity and dedicate himself to strengthening and reinterpreting the pillars of our Church to be relevant in the world of today, not the past?

The reasons appear to be evident:

- He does not consider change of any kind to be in his personal interest.
- Change is definitely not in the personal interest of his advisors, the Curia.

As a result, I believe that the Church is significantly worse off today than when we last saw the white smoke emerge from the Sistine Chapel. And worse yet is that it is 180 degrees off course. We can only hope for an early return of that white smoke announcing a far more enlightened decision. However, that may be too late.

Every Critical Catholic I have known has eventually come to the conclusion that change of any kind is so repugnant to the hierarchy that there is virtually no possibility for it to occur from the top down. It will never originate from the ornate Papal throne in St. Peter's. It must come from the plain pews of Catholic churches around the world.

So, there are a great many things about which all Catholics must do more than cope. Those who are Critical must continue to be militant and that is a tremendous challenge. They must call out their Compliant brethren and exhort them to become at least Curious. They must develop strategies to bring this about. Their Imitation of Christ must become that of Christ the Radical.

We all should be terrified that they might not succeed.

Chapter Two

The American Catholic

A 27-year old woman lay dying in a hospital in Phoenix, AZ. She was suffering from pulmonary hypertension, which interferes with the functioning of the heart and lungs. Pregnancy dramatically increases the risk of that disease and this young woman was eleven weeks pregnant with her fifth child. She was then in grave danger of death if her pregnancy were not terminated.

The facts of the matter were clear and simple:

- If the baby were taken at that point, since it was not yet viable, it would die.
- If nothing were done, the mother and therefore the baby would both die.
- If the pregnancy were terminated, the mother of four would probably recover.

The medical staff and the family anguished over their decision to abort and referred it to the Chairperson of the hospital's Ethics Committee, who happened to be on call. She concurred with the evaluation of the patient and the decision of the medical staff and the family to terminate the pregnancy. The woman recovered and returned home to her husband and four other children.

I am categorically opposed to abortion. In fact, my version of right to life extends to men and is stronger that many other Catholics, because it includes capital punishment and pre-emptive war.

In this case, I believe a sad and difficult decision was made, which was both rational and correct.

However, this was a Catholic Hospital and the Ethics Committee chairperson was a Sister of Mercy. More than six months after all this happened, the Bishop of Phoenix declared that the nun, all who participated in the decision (presumably including the woman's family) and all hospital personnel who assisted in any way in the procedure were excommunicated *latae sententiae*, that is, automatically and apparently retroactively.

I hope that was an equally sad and painfully difficult decision, but I am certain that it was both irrational and incorrect. It should be noted that abuse of children by priests does not merit *latae sententiae*, just reassignment.

The Bishop in his infinite wisdom also chose to make the tragedy a teaching moment, informing us that "an unborn child is not a disease". I consider that paternalistic rather than pastoral and very insulting.

But the Bishop was not through. On December 21, 2010, more than eighteen months after the heroic decision of the nun involved, Sister Margaret McBride, the Bishop declared the hospital to no longer be a Catholic institution.

Ironically, the hospital receives no financial support from the Diocese. The only practical effect of the Bishop severing ties with the hospital is that Mass cannot be celebrated there, which affects only the innocent. The old saying about cutting one's nose off to spite one's face comes to mind.

In a statement, St. Joseph's President Linda Hunt said it would comply with the Catholic leader's decision but defended itself, as follows: "If we are presented with a situation in which a pregnancy threatens a woman's life, our first priority is to save both patients. If that is not possible, we will always save the life we can save, and that is what we did in this case," Hunt said. "Morally, ethically, and legally, we simply cannot stand by and let someone die whose life we might be able to save."

Clearly, the policy stated by the hospital President describes not an elective abortion, but a morally sustainable medical treatment and that squares with my belief and my conscience. The Bishop and all who support his decision are wrong. I have been told by a friend who is a doctor that the real problem was in the placenta, not the fetus. Its removal, with the coincidental loss of the child in this case is even more consistent with Canon Law.

Fortunately, my belief is also held by a number of priests who are highly respected Canon lawyers. I suspect they will not be allowed to argue their case.

I would bet everything that I possess that within hours of making her decision, the nun involved in that situation, as would be any nun I ever knew, was with her Confessor and he absolved her of any *possible* sin involved. The validity of absolution is either a truth or not. I believe it is a truth and that she thereafter should not be liable for excommunication.

The Pope or some other responsible adult in the hierarchy should have immediately overruled the misguided Bishop and properly disciplined him. Automatic excommunication is wrong, but it is particularly egregious to an American Catholic, because it does not provide due process. While the Church is certainly not a democracy, this attitude flies in the face of our sense of fairness.

Make no mistake about it: the American Catholic is not just an idle righteous epithet, like "the Cafeteria Catholic". It is a reality and rightly so. The Roman Catholic Church must accept that reality or it may not continue to survive in the United States. That may sound like an ultimatum, but it is really merely an observation and one most thinking American Catholics would consider accurate.

This book is written from the perspective of American Catholics, whether describing them in the terms from an earlier book, Compliant, Curious or Critical. However, it is mostly about those *American* Catholics who are critical of their church, because it is only they who can save the Roman Catholic Church from irrelevance in America and perhaps throughout the world.

I believe that the reason American Catholics are unique in this regard is basically because since its inception, the United States has been free and a democracy and there is no other tradition. Therefore, the Church of Rome is the one who finds itself out of step.

Many of the immigrants who have come to the United States over the past more than two centuries have come here for just that reason, so this American mindset is generally accepted and treasured. Of course, most of those immigrants came from places where democracy was not the predominate tradition and in fact many came from overwhelmingly Catholic countries where for centuries secular traditions were not in conflict with the Church.

Until the middle of the last century many Catholics, because they came from poorer and middle class immigrant families, with no tradition of higher education were often not very sophisticated and accepted things pretty much the way they were presented.

Then along came the GI Bill and the education and opportunity that went with it. That was followed by the promise of Vatican II and then later in the sixties, when the validity of many institutions and beliefs were called into question. As those issues were raised rational answers were needed and often they were not forthcoming.

For the most part, the questions being asked by Catholics of their Church were not about the basic tenets of their Faith as outlined in the Creed, but about matters of governance and man-made rules and regulations, which affected their daily lives and their abilities to take care of their families.

For its part, unfortunately many of the answers coming from the Institutional Church were, "Because we say so", which is not tolerated at all well in a democracy. At first most Catholics were Compliant and went along with the situations, but gradually some became Curious about the underlying logic of these answers, the corruption of those in power, the way layperson's questions and concerns were ignored and the cavalier way in which they were treated for having asked.

Some of these Curious Catholics just gave up and left. Others like me stayed and have tried to be constructively Critical Catholics, hopeful that their efforts will bring about change. That has not been easy, nor has it been particularly effective.

Critical American Catholics have asked these difficult questions from the perspective of their democratic tradition. They are not just opposed to laws; they are proud to be citizens of a country of laws. They are equally proud of their tradition of separation between Church and State and its important corollary, the freedom to practice their religion.

They believe in due process, a concept not held in great esteem by the Church. They don't like ex post facto laws. They think people should be considered innocent until they are *proven* guilty and they think that punishment should fit the crime. They also feel they have the right of appeal.

They think the process of governance should be both transparent and fair without regard to gender, religious beliefs, status in the hierarchy, sexual or political orientation, or social status, or how much they contribute to the Church or any other extraneous consideration. And they don't like dumb laws.

They think automatic excommunication is an outrageous concept. They think that embarrassing a public official by withholding the sacraments is blackmail. They think that a Bishop who discovers a priest who is a pedophile should make a citizen's arrest and call the Sheriff. And they believe if he doesn't, he should be charged as an accessory before *and* after the fact.

Critical Catholics think the annulment process is obscure and demeaning. They think birth control decisions are matters for the individual consciences of the persons involved and not the business of the Institutional Church. They think that limiting the participation of women in the liturgy is discriminatory and wasteful of a desperately needed resource. They think a celibate clergy is unnatural and self-defeating.

They think that the failure of the Institutional Church to speak out on the <u>moral</u>, rather than the political issues of guaranteed universal health care, immigration policy, racism, unjust war, capital punishment, civil rights of homosexuals; as well as corruption in government, business, social services, unions and in the Institutional Church itself is malfeasance, in addition to being a disgrace.

American Catholics think this way because they are free people living in a democracy and they believe that is the way their institutions should act. It is an expression of <u>confidence</u> in their Church, not disrespect. The Institutional Church in turn owes them a willingness to adapt to this culture.

Such willingness has long been foreign to the Institutional Church. Catholic Church practice and tradition has been influenced by centuries of monarchial rule, under which Church and State operated in a complementary fashion, with a concomitant reduction in the freedom of citizen-parishioners.

It is not easy for anyone to live under conflicting philosophies of governance. That of a democracy is to adapt and grow without compromising one's basic principles. That once was the philosophy of the Catholic Church, but since Vatican I, it has been to force everyone else to adapt, to resist any change and to rule by intimidation, hearkening back to the Inquisition.

For more than a hundred fifty years, since Vatican I American Catholics have sighed, "Well that is the way of the Church and there is nothing that can be done about that". They have cut the Church more slack than it has sometime deserved. They have tried to explain as well as they could and apologize for their religion. Religion courses in Catholic Colleges have actually been titled "Apologetics".

Many American Catholics have left the Church because of these attitudes, although a majority of them still identify themselves as Catholics. However, many more American Catholics have stayed and continue to practice their religion, despite their objections to the way the Church treats them. They cope. Many cope by simply ignoring the Hierarchy which has lost their trust. A friend of mine describes this as schismatic-in-place.

Coping is the reluctant, if qualified acceptance of the status quo and therefore tacit approval of it. Those who cope have become part of the problem. They also do a disservice to their Faith and are complicit in the decline of the Catholic Church.

Chapter Three

The State of the Church

T he Roman Catholic Church is governed as a highly selective benevolent oligarchy, directed by the Pope and the Roman Curia, collectively referred to herein as the Vatican, under a mantle of implied infallibility. This oligarchy is selectively benevolent in the sense that the level of charitable works which the Catholic Church carries out all over the world is well known and properly acclaimed. At the same time the Institutional Church appears to be totally insensitive to and rather dismissive of the basic non-financial, human needs of millions of its members.

The concept of implied infallibility flows from proclamation of Vatican I just one hundred and fifty years ago that the Pope is infallible *when speaking about faith and morals under specific circumstances*. The doctrine of infallibility, whatever one believes about it, does not cover the governance or discipline of the Church, even though it is routinely applied.

This doctrine is one of the least understood by ordinary Catholics and many believe the Institutional Church has purposefully made no effort to clarify that lack of understanding. Therein is the power of implied infallibility or as noted Theologian Charles E. Curran calls it, "creeping infallibilism".

*****

Before we go any farther, let us take a brief look at the history of Infallibility. Author and reporter for Time Magazine in Rome during Vatican II Robert Blair Kaiser describes the reporting of one of his historical counterparts nearly one hundred years earlier in the Introduction to his book *A Church In Search Of Itself*, Vintage Books An Imprint of Random House, Inc., New York, March 2007, An important excerpt is as follows:

> "John Emerich Edward Dalberg the first Lord Acton...spent his most productive early years as a newspaper correspondent in Rome at the First Vatican Ecumenical Council in1869-70. Acton filed passionate reports on that Council's battle over papal infallibility...

> Acton, an English lord with blood ties to the nobility of two European nations, opposed any declaration of papal infallibility, convinced that Pope Pius IX was promoting it in order to shore up his temporal power...Acton not only reported on the debate inside this Council; he even wrote speeches for some of the bishops who were arguing against a declaration a declaration...When one of the bishops dared to tell the Pope that infallibility had no precedent in ancient Church tradition, Pius IX exploded. *Traditio sono io. Sono io la chiesa* is how he put it: 'I am tradition. I am the Church'.

> A third of the bishops (from the Council) fled Rome rather than to give this Pope the absolute power he wanted. Those who were left at the Council (547 of them) agreed with Pius IX's self-promotion and set the Church up for the papolatry that has bedeviled I ever since..."

Pius IX is the man who was in 2000 beatified by John Paul II, who himself is currently being "fast-tracked" to beatification by his trusted advisor Benedict XVI. There appears to be a rather self-serving pattern here.

Kaiser continues:

"Acton's dispatches...were reprinted all over the world under the pseudonym Quirinus. He wrote them in a hurry, often finishing them at 4 a.m. and smuggling them out of Rome via diplomatic pouch to avoid confiscation by the Pope's secret police. His reports warned the readers about the dangers of making the pope into some kind of god. But he did not have the final word. The Quirinus Collection, his account of the battle, was put on Rome's *Index of Forbidden Books* and its editor, Ignaz von Dollinger, the best German Theologian of the day was excommunicated."

It is perhaps ironic that today this same Lord Acton is best remembered for his famous quote regarding organizations in general: "Power corrupts and absolute power corrupts absolutely".

I could not find any information as to whether the vote for Infallibility was 547-0, but I do know that the number of those who left was not exactly one-third since that would be 273.5 people. If it had been 274 and they all voted no and all of those who stayed voted yes, the declaration would have failed under the rules of Vatican II.

Would that have meant that the Church would be better off today? I don't know, but I don't think it could be worse.

Regardless of this questionable provenance of Papal infallibility and your individual assessment of it, the relevance here is that today many Catholics think the Pope is infallible *in whatever he says or does*. Therefore, although Popes have only invoked infallibility twice in history and then on issues which have very little impact on ordinary human life or activity, when a Pope issues an encyclical or a strong statement on *any* issue, those

Catholics *feel* that he has spoken infallibly and react that way.

Compliant Catholics of course are the most accepting of this way of thinking. During the reign of John Paul II, the Congregation of the Faith, which was under the direction of Cardinal Ratzinger, now Benedict XVI was the primary beneficiary of this implied infallibility, which he generously shared with the rest of the Hierarchy. Of course, that was not his to use much less share, but the pattern continues.

Furthermore, since those Catholics believe that the Curia and the Pope almost by definition are in total agreement on everything, anything said by a Cardinal of the Curia is essentially considered infallible. And that isn't the end of it.

The media and unfortunately even the local Bishops usually refer to any pronouncements from the Pope, the Curia or anyone working in "the Papal household" as being *from the Vatican*, which those same Catholics mentioned above, consider as code for the Pope and therefore having been spoken or written infallibly. When you think about that, it is just human nature.

The activities and deliberations within this coalition of the Pope and the Curia are traditionally both opaque and secretive. There is no defined and working mechanism for them to even learn about the concerns and problems of the more than a billion Catholics worldwide and the Church apparently has no interest in doing anything about that. That is apparently satisfactory to the hierarchy because only rarely are these proclamations ever the subject of a series of homilies, their rationales are not explained and God forbid, they are never discussed widely.

Ironically, despite the preponderance of evidence that the Church is on a collision course with ultimate irrelevance, this leadership apparently feels it is not in their collective, vested, best interest for them to change the situation one iota. They are taking us all down with them.

There is even a widespread theory that the strategy of the leadership of the Institutional Church is to return it to the mode following Vatican I and to reduce its membership significantly by systematically alienating those who disagree, to the point at which they will all leave. Can you spell cult?

During and immediately after Vatican II there was much discussion of Magisterium, that is, the teaching authority of the Catholic Church. However, Magisterium as applied by the Vatican ignores the reality that effective teaching is an *interactive* process through dialogue. In practice, dialogue seems to be considered both undesirable and impertinent by the Church, despite its prominence in the documents of Vatican II.

Periodically, proclamations are issued with the expectation that they will be embraced and followed without questioning. There is no mechanism for appeal of these arbitrary decisions and no apparent effort is made to either explain or discuss them. As a result, in practice these documents are largely ignored by many Catholics, especially those of the "critical persuasion".

One would think that the cornerstone of Magisterium would be the bishops. After all, they are really the only ones outside of the Vatican who are allowed to ask questions, albeit at their peril.

One would also think that the bishops would develop plain and understandable explanations of the old as well as new doctrines and, most importantly how they affect average Catholics. They could then, conduct workshops for the pastors, which would include suggestions for homilies on the subject.

Obviously, this would promote dialogue and perhaps questioning or even criticism. However, that is the essence of education.

Along with a discussion of doctrine they could address the *moral* implications of national and local issues to enlighten the faithful so they can reason through the partisan politics. For example, during the health care debate, we could have used a few discussions on the *morality of denying health care to anyone because they cannot afford it.* Another interesting subject might be for the bishops to take a position on the *morality* underlying the entire Immigration issue instead of limiting their involvement to an appeal for funds to assist abused migrant workers and ineffective lip service to the causes such as porous borders, employers hiring illegal workers, the need for a national ID card and a path to citizenship for those already here who are qualified.

Certainly, all bishops must have plenty of time to do this. After all, there are four times as many Bishops in the United States as there are Governors and no one can tell me that the Governors don't have more difficult jobs. Besides, they must deal with legislators *and* run for re-election.

However, in the United States the impotent US Conference of Catholic Bishops vacillates between silence and inappropriate action on important issues like Universal Health Care, Immigration, clerical sexual abuse, rampant corruption among leaders of business and industry and unjust War. Occasionally, the Council releases a pompous pronouncement with little more than "here it is, believe it", which makes them sound like they all slept through the debate. It would be refreshing if once in a while they had a new idea instead of merely a new way to say "Thou shalt not" do, think or say something.

The impotence of the USCCB is not all self-imposed. All too often they are hobbled by the culpable equivocation of the Curia on issues such as the role of women in the Church and they have not demonstrated the courage to take a strong stand.

Many thinking Catholics are embarrassed by this. Many other thinking Catholics, including a few bishops and many pastors don't hold the USCCB in sufficient regard to be embarrassed by the process and just ignore it. Protecting pedophiles has that effect on credibility.

Most Catholics who were either taught to, or have decided to not think for themselves, merely accept the proclamations by the Conference. These latter are culpable and seriously complicit in the mess we have.

As a result of this pattern the bishops and the congregations they are supposed to serve are losing their voice in the public square. Instead of being constructive on the issues per se, some bishops showboat for their own aggrandizement by refusing the sacraments to elected officials who, although personally opposed to abortion, faithfully represent the views of their constituents *as they are sworn to do* by the Constitution. Is an oath not binding? As a group, the Bishops *just don't get democracy* and are clueless as to how to operate in it.

Part of this situation is due to the organizational structure of the Church. Theoretically, the bishops are the operational managers of the faithful. There are more than 5,000 bishops in the Latin and Eastern wings of the Catholic Church and virtually all of them were hand-picked by the current Pope and appointed by his predecessor.

They each report directly to the Pope. There is no even vaguely similar organizational structure in the world, with such a span of control. And it simply cannot work.

Each of those more than five thousand bishops is required to meet with his "boss" for fifteen minutes on *once every five years* for what is called their ad limina visit. For many of them, that is their only contact with their direct supervisor. What do you suppose they talk about? My guess is very little that relates to anything in this book.

When their allotted time with the boss is finished, they shuffle off to the Curia to be told what to believe and receive their official orders. These men are the only contact between the Church as described by John XXIII as all of us and the Institutional Church as described by Cardinal Dulles. No wonder it doesn't work.

How many times in the past six years do you suppose a bishop has mentioned the beliefs of many Catholics about birth control or stem cell research to the Pope in one of those meetings? My uninformed guess is never and I would bet on it.

Currently, the schedule for ad limina visits managed by the Vatican is running about a year behind. There is just not enough time to see everyone. Not a way to run a railroad and definitely not a way to run a Church with more than a billion members.

The bishops obviously do not serve as advocates or representatives of the faithful in the pews. They do not provide a communications link upwards to transmit the ideas, concerns and needs of the masses of Catholics who need and are entitled to one. There is no defined path available to ordinary laypeople for this and apparently there is no interest by the hierarchy of the Church in establishing one. One might conclude that the Institutional Church would actively oppose any effort by those ordinary laypeople to establish such a communications channel.

Thinking American Catholics cannot understand how these same bishops can arbitrarily reassign pedophiles, but are not able or willing to exert enough pressure on the Vatican to alleviate the shortage of priests, even if it means eliminating celibacy or ordaining women...or both.

In a recent address in Ireland, well-known Catholic author, Robert Blair Kaiser mentioned above and about whom you will hear much more in a later chapter had this to say:

"The most significant actions of Benedict's papacy so far have had nothing to do with his priests and bishops: he has set in motion two investigations of American nuns, one of them a doctrinal inquiry by the pope's heresy-hunting department. Will this be the pope's Final Solution to the problem of his uppity American nuns? Condemnation by the Holy Office of the Inquisition? (In my humble opinion, our nuns, the bravest, most generous Jesus-people in the universe, should be investigating the Vatican.)"

Once again, I am absolutely and categorically opposed to abortion (although I agree that legalizing it undoubtedly made it safer) and the other forms of murder the Institutional Church finds more comfortable, such as the execution of criminals, even though some bishops have outspoken in their opposition to the death penalty and the waging of unjust wars. However, I believe that my time and efforts are better spent trying to right wrongs where I might be more successful (which is why I am writing this book), than participating in demonstrations against a Court decision with no chance of reversal.

Many wonder why the Church cannot just accept that the battle to outlaw abortion in this country has long ago been lost forever. They seem incapable of accepting that it is the law of the land, condemning the act as murder, moving on and channeling those efforts to something on which they can make a difference. They also cannot understand why approval of an abortion to save the life of the mother as in the recent case cited earlier warrants "automatic excommunication" but child abuse, execution of criminals, unjust wars and cold blooded, premeditated murder do not.

In my perhaps cynical opinion, the apparent preoccupation with legalized abortion may merely be a contrived means of distraction for the people in the pews to keep them from doing something more constructive.

*****

Thinking Catholics wonder why their voices are not heard. Notice that I said they are not heard, because no one is *listening* and if by chance they are, those voices are ignored. That was what collegiality, removed from the agenda of Vatican II by Paul VI, was all about.

The reason is simple. The bishops are willingly or not, part of a ruse that collegiality actually exists when in fact the Vatican cares not a whit about what we think. Who is kidding whom?

Since changes in the way the Institutional Church does business will never come from the top down, any changes and remedies must come from the bottom up. Unfortunately at least at the present, it would seem that the only ones left who are interested in any kind of change are the informed Critical Catholics.

It is an almost impossible task for the Critical Catholics to bring about any change for two reasons:

- Since many informed Critical Catholics have long ago given up and left, the majority of Catholics who are practicing members of the Church are Compliant Catholics.
- Almost all Compliant Catholics are incurious, therefore uninformed and perhaps culpably igno-rant, which is defined as lacking the knowledge or understanding *that results from the omission of ordinary care to acquire such knowledge or understanding.*

While writing this book I have been surprised at the number of things I have learned about the historical governance of the Church I thought I knew so well. However, I am *astounded* at the staggering number of Compliant Catholics who are uninformed or misinformed and don't care.

Most of them would undoubtedly rather say that they are *traditional* Catholics, but that would not be accurate if it means they are the *only* traditional Catholics. I am also a traditional Catholic; an acceptor of the truths found in the Apostle's and Nicene Creeds; a believer in the power of the Eucharist; a follower of Jesus Christ and a beneficiary of the Holy Spirit.

However, I arrived at my Faith intellectually as well as spiritually. I maintain a level of intellectual curiosity about many things, including my religion. I am a traditional Catholic who is critical because I am both curious and informed. One might argue that I am a Catholic because of my Faith rather than my religion and that is probably true. I have always been curious about things that interest and affect me. My Catholicism qualifies on both counts.

That intellectual curiosity has led me to question and find lacking many elements of Catholicism having to do with the organization, administration and governance of the Catholic Church, separate from its dogma and doctrines. I am a traditional Catholic, but one who is also Critical.

Back in the day, each September when we returned to school (that is really "back in the day" for me), we usually started with one or more new notebooks. I recall that mine usually had a shield with a coat-of-arms on them emblazoned with the principle: "Knowledge is Power". That was to motivate us. As I grew older I realized that the corollary of that principle, "Ignorance is Subservience" might have been a stronger motivation.

Taken together those two statements are elegant in their simplicity and symmetry. The underlying truth is equally symmetrical. The difference between knowledge and ignorance is curiosity and the difference between power and subservience is compliance. If one is compliant, one is not curious.

What about, then these Traditional Catholics who are doggedly Compliant? What are the characteristics which define them?

There is no doubt that they are basically good people trying to do the right thing. However, they willingly embrace whatever they are told regarding what their Religion requires of them and often it doesn't matter who it was who told them. They live in fear of somehow breaking some Church law they do not know about and therefore often act in an overabundance of scrupulousness. In that sense, they live in a world of fear.

Their world is one without any doubt except that they may not be religious enough. They thrive on certitude, wherever they can find it and without questioning its source or its validity.

These traditional Catholics are diligent in the search for constant reassurance concerning their Compliance, subscribing to the same kinds of magazines their parents used to read, like the *Catholic Answer* and *the St. Anthony Messenger* in which every situation is portrayed in startlingly intense black and dazzling white. On the other hand, they would never buy a copy of *The National Catholic Reporter, Commonweal, America* or *US Catholic*, which they treat as occasions of sin, whatever that is.

They tend to associate mostly with other traditional Catholics, perhaps in some cases because they have not intellectually equipped themselves to handle any debate on the simplest religious issue. That is part of the problem, since they are rarely confronted with an opposing position.

When asked what the source is of a specific belief, they don't know and they are often unaware of the history behind most Institutional Church positions. In other cases it may be that after so many years they find it difficult to even think about questioning or being critical of the Institutional Church which has been so important to them and such a significant part of their lives.

When told by some well meaning Catholic what I should believe, or do or oppose I always ask them how they know that. I am often amazed that the source is merely an acquaintance who mentioned it and they have made no personal effort to verify the statement.

This is not to say that Compliant Catholics have limited intellects, because that is not the case with many I have met. They are simply not curious. How do I know that? I know it because if they had even the most elementary level of curiosity, they could not resist being critical at least once in a while.

As a result this lack of curiosity, they are extremely vulnerable to the lunatic fringe of our Faith, such as some fervent followers of:

- The Legionaries of Christ (their website avoids any reference to the problems of founder Father Maciel, except for a brief mention "May 2006– the Congregation for the Doctrine of the Faith, after a mature examination of accusations brought forward against Father Maciel, invited him to "a reserved life of prayer and penance, renouncing all public ministry.") Actually, Father Maciel was found to have sexually abused as many as twenty seminarians and others and to have fathered as many as eight children by three different women, for which he was never punished. Nice guy.
- The Slaves of the Immaculate Heart of Mary (isn't that a lovely image? The Blessed Mother as slave owner. Welcome to the Church of St. Mary's Plantation.) This group was founded by the excommunicated and then in 1972 strangely "reconciled" (by Paul VI) Father Leonard Feeney, SJ. They are lobbying for a return to the Tridentine Mass and the

discredited Feeney dogma of "outside the Church there is no salvation". There is progress for you.

- Opus Dei (a personal prelature of the Pope, reporting directly to him. There are not any other prelatures, nor have there ever been before). This group has many dangerous, sick ideas and cult-like practices. Not a good thing for the incurious and poorly informed to encounter, which probably is the reason for their limited success.

Compliant Catholics would never initiate a discussion about Church law or practice. Many of them do not realize that most of the policies and practices which affect them on a daily basis are man-made, not based in scripture or tradition and often have only a tenuous relationship with matters of faith. Remember the requirement to eat fish on Friday? (Ironically, many Compliant Catholics don't know that the Friday regulation had nothing to do with fish. The requirement was to abstain from meat from a warm blooded animal. Fish was an acceptable alternative, but not required fare.)

Compliant Catholics are resolutely uninformed about two things: The Church has operated very well in the same way, for 2,000 years and Vatican II was the worst thing that ever happened to it.

Unless something unimaginable forces the issue, these traditional and Compliant Catholics are never going to help change the way the Institutional Church manages or governs. As a result, the Church will continue losing members, it will cease to be relevant and they will be the only ones left.

The greatest irony of this impending collapse of the Catholic Church is that the blame for it lies not with those who have left, but with those who did not. It has taken a long time for the losses of members to reach critical mass (no pun intended) but it finally is approaching.

Compliant Catholics have become *complicit* in the collapse. So have the Critical Catholics who are willing to cope. They are among the villains in the fall of the Church, not the heroes fighting the good fight. In a very real sense, they have become complicit in the failure of that to which they are trying to cling.

I believe that it could be argued that the Critical Catholics who are complicit are perhaps *more* culpable because they have been curious, have discovered the truth and have not called out their Compliant fellow parishioners. There is plenty of blame to go around.

Since the defection of Martin Luther and the ensuing Reformation, the leadership of the Church has used their power and the fear of damnation to insist on both loyalty and the preservation of the status quo. Ignorance is their strongest ally. The long and the short of it is that the leadership of the Institutional Church, from the Pope down through the Bishops has demanded a higher level of responsibility on the part of the Laity for their behavior than they have required of themselves. I find no justification for that policy.

This is a complete lack of basic leadership and if there is to be any hope at all, that must change.

For Catholics who are Critical, the only way for them to avoid also being equally complicit with their Compliant brethren is to awake the innate curiosity of those who are Compliant, educate them in the history of the Church, good and bad; show them the wisdom of Vatican II and demonstrate how they are being misled.

Compliance must be challenged and it has been my experience that when one does that logically and without prejudice, educated Compliant Catholics accept that rather well. It is also been my experience that many Compliant Catholics are painfully unaware of some basic truths about their religion. Most of their knowledge is second or third hand, often from unreliable or uniformed or perhaps dishonest sources.

Ironically, when they discover they have in fact been duped, they are angry and, at least in part accept some of the responsibility.

Compliance often comes down to a steadfast belief in two myths: The Church is operating today in the same way as it has for 2,000 years and that has a long history of success; The problems facing the Church today are the sole and direct result of Vatican II in which a few devious people were able make terrible and widespread changes despite the will of the majority of the Church.

We will deal with those two myths in later chapters (two each), hopefully encouraging the Compliant Catholics who read them to become more curious and to learn the truth, and inspiring Critical Catholics to challenge the beliefs of those who are Compliant.

Chapter Four

Myth One: The Historical (In) Consistency of the Church

"The Church has operated in the same way, by the same rules for 2,000 years and it has done just fine". Both parts of that proclamation are, of course inaccurate. However, when I engage fellow Catholics who are Compliant or traditional in their beliefs in conversations about the need for reform and changes in the governance and discipline of the Church, that is the usual response.

The facts are that *prior to the past hundred and fifty years* governance and discipline in the Church was *not* consistent and predictable, but adaptive and responsive, albeit often agonizingly slow to respond. Ironically, the *consistency* of the past hundred and fifty years has been catastrophic and those who think that the Church is really doing "just fine", are delusional.

In this chapter we will examine how much the organization and governance and discipline of the Catholic Church has changed over the course of those two thousand years. This is a daunting task because for most of that period even the inconsistency has been inconsistent.

We will rely as a primary reference on *The Church: The Evolution of Catholicism* by Rev. Richard P. McBrien a renowned Ecclesiologist from the Faculty of the University of Notre Dame. This book, copyrighted in 2008 was published by HarperOne an imprint of Harper Collins Publishing of New York City.

According to Father McBrien, "Ecclesiology is literally...the Theological study of the Church, which studies the Church as a mystery or sacrament". It is not therefore strictly an historical account of events, nor is it concerned with matters of governance and discipline. It is rather, a study of the dynamics of its evolution; the path of its philosophical strategy.

We begin with the Church, if we could call it that, in the years immediately following the time of Christ. Here we find a small band of uneducated, unsophisticated, somewhat terrified Apostles, with one of their members being hastily recruited to replace a traitor and another who had expressed serious doubts about the whole underlying concept.

They augmented their numbers significantly, tenfold in fact, with promising fellow believers who were no doubt eager to get out of Jerusalem after the recent unpleasantness. Equipped only with their first or in some cases second hand knowledge of Christ, they set off in different directions following a business model that was a precursor of Amway.

These were the closest observers of and witnesses to the establishment of what might become the Christian Church and the only documentation of their stories is recorded in the fifth book of the New Testament, The Acts of the Apostles. Their level of success was remarkable, if not miraculous.

In its article on the Acts of the Apostles, The Catholic Encyclopedia describes this beginning period of the Church, opening with the disclaimer that "The book does not contain the Acts of all the Apostles neither does it contain all the acts of any Apostle". Then it meticulously documents the principal known events of the early Church.

I recommend that you read that article in full. However, for the purposes of this book, I will summarize the parts of it that are relevant to this chapter, setting up the point I want to make.

In the days immediately following the Resurrection Peter, aided by the Holy Spirit and assisted by John reorganized the original twelve Apostles, who soon discovered that through the Holy Spirit they had extraordinary and very useful powers of language and healing. They did not consider themselves Christians, but Jews to whom the long awaited Messiah had been revealed. They believed their mission was to enlighten their fellow Jews and thereby gain some advantage over their occupiers, the Romans.

The message of the Apostles and their companions was embraced by many of the Jews of Jerusalem, despite the fact that a few short weeks earlier they had concurred with the decision to put that Messiah to death. Their local numbers grew quickly to a reported five thousand men. The number of women and children was not reported, but it can probably be assumed to increase the total numbers to more than ten thousand.

This success did not escape the notice of the Jewish leaders, who considered the Apostles a threat to their authority. Peter and John were arrested and called to account for their actions.

The two early leaders quickly developed a new strategy. They appointed leaders from their numbers as Bishops to lead those in Jerusalem who had already been converted and to attract additional followers. Then Peter and John focused their attention on expanding their market to Jews elsewhere in the Roman Empire, including those in Rome itself.

However, before they set forth, playing to the enthusiasm of the newly converted, Peter and John conducted the first known fundraising effort for the missions. The response was generally overwhelming. Many of their followers sold their homes and contributed the proceeds to the cause, although the first known instance of fundraising graft emerged.

> "...a certain Ananias, with Saphira his wife, sold a possession and kept back part of the price, the wife being accessory to the deed. St. Peter is inspired by the Holy Ghost to know the deception, and rebukes Ananias for the lie to the Holy Ghost. At the rebuke the man falls dead. Saphira, coming up afterwards, and knowing nothing of the death of her husband, is interrogated by St. Peter regarding the transaction. She also keeps back a part of the price, and lying asserts that the full price has been brought to the Apostles. St. Peter rebukes her, and she also falls dead at his words."

So much for due process in the early Church.

Peter and John realized that they had clearly outlived their welcome in the area. We are told they selected a corps of 120 believers to take their message to Jews in the surrounding area.

This band of zealots, struck out with just the clothes on their backs. Since we know that several of the original twelve were married, we can probably assume that a similar percentage of the other hundred and eight were as well and that they took their families with them. No, the original clergy was not celibate and yes, some of those 120 may have actually been women.

Meanwhile, Saul later to be called Paul, a loyalist to the Jewish hierarchy was busy persecuting all those who had accepted the news of the Messiah. We are all familiar with the story of what happened to him while he was in his way to Damascus to deal with that community's believers. It resulted in his conversion and his decision to take the message of Christ to the Gentiles, with his deputy Barnabas. Almost immediately, a problem arose that no one had anticipated.

The Gentiles who were mostly Greeks, balked at being required to embrace the Mosaic Law with its dietary constraints and even more strongly its practice of circumcision, which was not their custom. It apparently had not occurred to the Apostles that those requirements might be a serious impediment for their non-Jewish candidates for recruitment. Since Paul was preaching to this new vision specifically to the Gentiles, this was a significant problem.

Christ had not specifically allowed his followers to defy or even relax the requirements of Mosaic Law, since that possibility had not been anticipated. This precipitated a dispute between Peter and Paul sometimes described as "the incident at Antioch" in which Paul challenged the requirement. After having a vision concerning clean and unclean foods, Peter agreed that the rule should be waived at a meeting later called the Council at Jerusalem. I wonder if Peter thought he was infallible. I doubt that Paul did. Or did those two soldiers in the field just agree to decide and "git 'er done!"

One might argue that with that agreement, Christianity became a stand-alone religion and no longer a sub-sect of Judaism. In any event, the pagan Gentiles began calling the converts "Christians", not Jews.

Some Theologians have questioned whether, despite saying "You are the rock on which I will build my Church" Christ intended to found a Church or merely update Judaism with the news of the coming of the Messiah and then take that message to the all non-Jews, converting them to Judaism. They also point out that according to scriptural literalists as a man, Jesus thought the world would end soon and clearly neither he nor the Apostles were aware of entire civilizations in the Far East and the Americas. Therefore, the idea of establishing a new religion may never have occurred to them.

This is an important point, since Judaism has never been a missionary religion determined to convert others. For that matter, Christ did not venture very far in the brief three years of His ministry. It may be that before Paul entered the picture that the plan was merely for the Apostles to convince all the Jews in the immediate area that Christ was the Messiah. In that case, there mission would have been "Go and teach *the Jews in* all nations".

In his book *The Church*, Father McBrien deals with the question of Christ's intention this way:

"The answer to the question of whether Jesus intended to "found" a church is no, if by "found we mean some direct, explicit, deliberate act by which Jesus established a new religious community and organization. This view is known as *precritical*, or what the late New Testament scholar Raymond E. Brown (d. 1998) called a 'blueprint ecclesiology'

The answer is yes, if by 'found' we mean 'lay the foundations for' the church in various indirect ways, that is, by the gathering of the apostles, which set him apart from the rabbis of his days, and by the establishment of a communal meal in direct continuity with the Eucharist, which Vatican II's Constitution on the Sacred Liturgy regards as 'the summit toward which the activity of the church is directed [and] the source from which all its power flows' (n. 10).

In the latter case, it would be preferable to speak of the church as having its *origin* in Jesus rather than as having been directly and explicitly founded by him. In contrast, this view is known as *historic-critical*. According to Daniel Harrington in *The Church According to the New Testament*:

It has recently become customary in academic circles to refer to the Jesus movement. The term refers to the public ministry of Jesus of Nazareth and the impact it had on other people. The term captures the dynamism that Jesus and his first followers displayed as they moved about the land of Israel and proclaimed the kingdom of God. Conversely, it avoids the static and institutional connotations that are often attached to the word church. *And it leaves open whether it is proper to speak of "the church" prior to Jesus' death and resurrection."*

Be that as it may, it was now time to regionalize, with Peter and John concentrating on the Jews and Paul and Barnabas pursuing the Gentiles, which would eventually include the Romans. Clearly they were inspired by the Holy Spirit and benefitted from Divine Guidance.

However, it is important to realize that these 120 missionaries and their successors carried no promotional material and had no brochures or any supply of tchotchkes to leave behind. Not even a small cross on a chain.

Everything there was to know about this new Faith was in the heads of these dedicated apostles and disciples and it was mostly spread by word of mouth. Anyone who has played that parlor game, in which someone whispers something to the person next to him or her and it is repeated around the circle, knows how well that works out, even with the help of the Holy Spirit.

How much you believe that what they saw and were told by Jesus they retained accurately, explained clearly and was remembered correctly depends on your belief in the power of the Holy Spirit. I definitely believe in that power, but I don't believe in the absolute memory retention of millions of people over thousands of years. Besides, before Gutenberg, each copy of any documentation available was subject to the interpretation of the scribe making the copy.

Logic tells us that these dedicated evangelists must have made up some details of the Faith as they ran into unanticipated questions and "what ifs" about which they had never thought or raised with Christ. It seems problematic that, widely dispersed as they were, they all agreed on those details.

These missionaries traveled separately for the most part and the plan was to carry the message of Christ beyond Jerusalem to Jews in neighboring cities and try to convert that community. These new Christians would then convert their friends, who would then in turn convert their friends and so on. Just like Amway.

When the time felt right and by their own individual decisions, the Apostles moved on to a new city, leaving a leader in the previous one in charge as a sort of early bishop. Some of them kept in touch with those leaders as well as they could and revisited them occasionally, but their emphasis was on spreading the word about Jesus to as many people as they could in the time they had. They could clean up the details over time.

When these bishops of the enclaves died, *the people of the area chose a successor* and the process continued. No one had the means or felt the need to check everything with Peter or any of his successors. Those were simpler days indeed.

We know from the letters of Paul that some of those enclaves occasionally went off track and the "bishops" had to be reminded of their errors. Surely some of those congregations must have failed and gone back to their old ways, or at least significantly modified what they had been told.

All of this goes to the question as to how consistently the message and the spirit of Christ's teachings were delivered and accepted in the early days of the Church. The point of all of this is that despite the power of the Holy Spirit, for more than three hundred years, with the difficulties of communications at the time and the limited documented direct interaction among those who were spreading the message, the consistency and the universality of the dogma and doctrines of this new Church seems quite problematic. Hence, heresies arose and flourished, sometimes for decades or more. There were also many heresies which developed, faded and no one ever was aware.

If one accepts the conventional duration of a generation as twenty-five years, this model for the Church lasted more than eleven generations, most of them under the siege of persecution. One must wonder how precisely the Christianity of the end of that period resembled the teaching of Christ as recounted in the Gospels of Matthew, Mark, Luke and John.

Assuming the Holy Spirit had been monitoring the situation closely, the basics were no doubt intact. However, it would seem logical that some, if not considerable amounts of extraneous, perhaps incorrect teachings had worked themselves into the message. The message probably needed a careful examination and perhaps revision. Consistency needed to be established.

Then in the early fourth century, two things happened. In 313, the Edict of Milan was issued, which Father McBrien describes as follows:

"After a long period of persecution, the Emperor Constantine accorded the Church not only the protection of the state, but favors and privileges as well. The clergy became, in effect civil servants...the Church became too closely identified with and dependent upon the political establishment..."

Pertinent to this discussion is that the Edict of Milan gave rise to opposition in the form of a movement called Monasticism, in which priests and religious retreated from the worldly side of the Church to monasteries where they reflected on and defined the fundamental elements of the Christian Faith. One result was the emergence of St. Augustine, the first of the four original Doctors of the Church.

A short twelve years later in 325, the First Ecumenical Council was convened. Here is the entry from the Catholic Encyclopedia article about Councils:

First Ecumenical Council: Nicaea I (325)
The Council of Nicaea lasted two months and twelve days. Three hundred and eighteen bishops were present. Hosius, Bishop of Cordova, assisted as legate of Pope Sylvester. The Emperor Constantine was also present. To this council we owe The Creed (*Symbolum*) of Nicaea, defining against Arius the true Divinity of the Son of God (*homoousios*), and the fixing of the date for keeping Easter (against the Quartodecimans).

There are several interesting elements to this entry:

- The Pope did not attend, but the Emperor did.
- It had been nearly 300 years before Christians decided they should codify their beliefs in a Creed (there was a prior "Apostles' Creed", which was written long after all the Apostles were all dead and of questionable provenance).
- It took a similar amount of time to define the Divinity of Jesus Christ and fix the date for Easter.
- It only lasted two months and twelve days as opposed to Vatican II, which lasted four years.

The attendance of the Emperor is of particular note. Most theologians believe that he convened the Council in order to standardize the Faith, which was probably a very good idea. The irony is that the Emperor caused it to happen, not the Pope.

The larger significance is that this marked the beginning of what became a very heavy-handed involvement of a series of Emperors of the Holy Roman Empire in the governance and discipline of the Church. That involvement led to a series of embarrassments including a period when there were three people claiming to be Pope; the ill-conceived Crusades; the defection of Martin

Luther and the start of the Protestant Reformation; Popes with mistresses and illegitimate children; and the Inquisitions.

The relationship lasted a thousand years until the Holy Roman Empire was abolished by its last Emperor, Francis II of Austria in 1806.

Detailing those events is beyond the scope of this book, but there is a wealth of historical data on these subjects available to the curious.

The fact is that today's Church dogma, doctrine and practices are at least in part an evolved collection of expedient actions by Ecumenical Councils, usually taken too late to deal with some crisis, and then imposed for eternity even after the crisis has passed.

The Catholic Encyclopedia includes two to eight line summaries of all the other Ecumenical Councils preceding Vatican II, as follows:

Second Ecumenical Council: Constantinople I (381)
The First General Council of Constantinople, under Pope Damasus and the Emperor Theodosius I, was attended by 150 bishops. It was directed against the followers of Macedonius, who impugned the Divinity of the Holy Ghost. To the above-mentioned Nicene Creed it added the clauses referring to the Holy Ghost (*qui simul adoratur*) and all that follows to the end.

Third Ecumenical Council: Ephesus (431)
The Council of Ephesus, of more than 200 bishops, presided over by St. Cyril of Alexandria representing Pope Celestine I, defined the true personal unity of Christ, declared Mary the Mother of God (*theotokos*) against Nestorius, Bishop of Constantinople, and renewed the condemnation of Pelagius.

Fourth Ecumenical Council: Chalcedon (451)
The Council of Chalcedon — 150 bishops under Pope Leo the Great and the Emperor Marcian — defined the two natures (Divine and human) in Christ against Eutyches, who was excommunicated.

Fifth Ecumenical Council: Constantinople II (553)
The Second General Council of Constantinople, of 165 bishops under Pope Vigilius and Emperor Justinian I, condemned the errors of Origen and certain writings (The Three Chapters) of Theodoret, of Theodore, Bishop of Mopsuestia and of Ibas, Bishop of Edessa; it further confirmed the first four general councils, especially that of Chalcedon whose authority was contested by some heretics.

The founder of Islam, Mohammed died in 663 and the Islamic religion emerged as something with which to be reckoned.

Sixth Ecumenical Council: Constantinople III (680-681)
The Third General Council of Constantinople, under Pope Agatho and the Emperor Constantine Pogonatus, was attended by the Patriarchs of Constantinople and of Antioch, 174 bishops, and the emperor. It put an end to Monothelitism by defining two wills in Christ, the Divine and the human, as two distinct principles of operation. It anathematized Sergius, Pyrrhus, Paul, Macarius, and all their followers.

Seventh Ecumenical Council: Nicaea II (787)
The Second Council of Nicaea was convoked by Emperor Constantine VI and his mother Irene, under Pope Adrian I, and was presided over by the legates of Pope Adrian; it regulated the veneration of holy images. Between 300 and 367 bishops assisted.

Eighth Ecumenical Council: Constantinople IV (869)
The Fourth General Council of Constantinople, under Pope Adrian II and Emperor Basil numbering 102 bishops, 3 papal legates, and 4 patriarchs, consigned to the flames the Acts of an irregular council (*conciliabulum*) brought together by Photius against Pope Nicholas and Ignatius the legitimate Patriarch of Constantinople; it condemned Photius who had unlawfully seized the patriarchal dignity. The Photian Schism, however, triumphed in the Greek Church, and no other general council took place in the East.

In 1054 the Pope and the Patriarch of Constantinople excommunicated each other kicking off the East-West Schism and the establishing the Orthodox Christian Church.

The First Crusade took place from 1095 through 1101.

Ninth Ecumenical Council: Lateran I (1123)
The First Lateran Council, the first held at Rome, met under Pope Callistus II. About 900 bishops and abbots assisted. It abolished the right claimed by lay princes, of investiture with ring and crosier to ecclesiastical benefices and dealt with church discipline and the recovery of the Holy Land from the infidels.

Tenth Ecumenical Council: Lateran II (1139)
The Second Lateran Council was held at Rome under Pope Innocent II, with an attendance of about 1000 prelates and the Emperor Conrad. Its object was to put an end to the errors of Arnold of Brescia.

The Second Crusade took place from 1145 through 1147.

Eleventh Ecumenical Council: Lateran III (1179)
The Third Lateran Council took place under Pope Alexander III, Frederick I being emperor. There were 302 bishops present. It condemned the Albigenses and Waldenses and issued numerous decrees for the reformation of morals.

The Third Crusade took place from 1188 through 1192. The Fourth was in 1204.

Twelfth Ecumenical Council: Lateran IV (1215)
The Fourth Lateran Council was held under Innocent III. There were present the Patriarchs of Constantinople and Jerusalem, 71 archbishops, 412 bishops, and 800 abbots the Primate of the Maronites, and St. Dominic. It issued an enlarged creed (symbol) against the Albigenses (Firmiter credimus), condemned the Trinitarian errors of Abbot Joachim, and published 70 important reformatory decrees.

This is the most important council of the Middle Ages, and it marks the culminating point of ecclesiastical life and papal power.

The Fifth Crusade took place in 1217. The Sixth ran from 1228 through 1239. The Inquisition began in 1231, with the acquiescence at least of Pope Innocent III.

Thirteenth Ecumenical Council: Lyons I (1245)

The First General Council of Lyons was presided over by Innocent IV; the Patriarchs of Constantinople, Antioch, and Aquileia (Venice), 140 bishops, Baldwin II, Emperor of the East, and St. Louis, King of France, assisted. It excommunicated and deposed Emperor Frederick II and directed a new crusade, under the command of St. Louis, against the Saracens and Mongols.

The Seventh Crusade lasted from 1249 through 1252. The last was in 1270.

Fourteenth Ecumenical Council: Lyons II (1274)

The Second General Council of Lyons was held by Pope Gregory X, the Patriarchs of Antioch and Constantinople, 15 cardinals, 500 bishops, and more than 1000 other dignitaries. It effected a temporary reunion of the Greek Church with Rome. The word *filioque* was added to the symbol of Constantinople and means were sought for recovering Palestine from the Turks. It also laid down the rules for papal elections.

Fifteenth Ecumenical Council: Vienne (1311-1313)

The Council of Vienne was held in that town in France by order of Clement V, the first of the Avignon popes. The Patriarchs of Antioch and Alexandria, 300 bishops (114 according to some authorities), and 3 kings — Philip IV of France, Edward II of England, and James II of Aragon — were present. The synod dealt with the crimes and errors imputed to the Knights Templars, the Fraticelli, the Beghards, and the Beguines, with projects of a new crusade, the reformation of the clergy, and the teaching of Oriental languages in the universities.

From 1378 until 1403 there were two Popes. In 1403 the Ecumenical Council at Pisa was convened to resolve the situation. Since it merely produced a third Pope, that Council was declared de facto illegal(?). Nonetheless, for thirty-six years the Church had multiple Popes at the same time.

Sixteenth Ecumenical Council: Constance (1414-1418)
The Council of Constance was held during the great Schism of the West, with the object of ending the divisions in the Church. It became legitimate only when Gregory XI had formally convoked it. Owing to this circumstance it succeeded in putting an end to the schism by the election of Pope Martin V, which the Council of Pisa (1403) had failed to accomplish on account of its illegality. The rightful pope confirmed the former decrees of the synod against Wyclif and Hus. This council is thus ecumenical only in its last sessions (XLII-XLV inclusive) and with respect to the decrees of earlier sessions approved by Martin V.

Seventeenth Ecumenical Council: Basle/Ferrara/ Florence (1431-1439)
The Council of Basle met first in that town, Eugene IV being pope, and Sigismund Emperor of the Holy Roman Empire. Its object was the religious pacification of Bohemia. Quarrels with the pope having arisen, the council was transferred first to Ferrara (1438), then to Florence (1439), where a short-lived union with the Greek Church was effected, the Greeks accepting the council's definition of controverted points. The Council of Basle is only ecumenical till the end of the twenty-fifth session, and of its decrees Eugene IV approved only such as dealt with the extirpation of heresy, the peace of Christendom, and the reform of the Church, and which at the same time did not derogate from the rights of the Holy See. (See also the Council of Florence.)

Eighteenth Ecumenical Council: Lateran V (1512-1517)
The Fifth Lateran Council sat from 1512 to 1517 under Popes Julius II and Leo X, the emperor being Maximilian I. Fifteen cardinals and about eighty archbishops and bishops took part in it. Its decrees are chiefly disciplinary. A new crusade against the Turks was also planned, but came to

naught, owing to the religious upheaval in Germany caused by Luther.

The "religious upheaval in Germany caused by Luther" was in fact his nailing of the 95 Theses on the door of All Saints Church in Wittenberg in 1517 and the start of the Protestant Reformation. They didn't get around to dealing with Martin Luther for another twenty-eight years.

In 1534, Henry VIII of England withdrew the Anglican Church from communion with the Pope.

The Holy Office of Rome, the first of the Congregations of the Curia was established in 1542 to take charge of the Inquisitions, which had been going on, out of control for more than three hundred years. It certainly was time for a little adult supervision, but there was little improvement.

Nineteenth Ecumenical Council: Trent (1545-1563)
The Council of Trent lasted eighteen years (1545-1563) under five popes: Paul III, Julius III, Marcellus II, Paul IV and Pius IV, and under the Emperors Charles V and Ferdinand. There were present 5 cardinal legates of the Holy See, 3 patriarchs, 33 archbishops, 235 bishops, 7 abbots, 7 generals of monastic orders, and 160 doctors of divinity. It was convoked to examine and condemn the errors promulgated by Luther and other Reformers, and to reform the discipline of the Church. Of all councils it lasted longest, issued the largest number of dogmatic and reformatory decrees, and produced the most beneficial results.

Twentieth Ecumenical Council: Vatican I (1869-1870)
The Vatican Council was summoned by Pius IX. It met 8 December, 1869, and lasted till 18 July, 1870, when it was adjourned; it is still unfinished. There were present 6 archbishop-princes, 49 cardinals, 11 patriarchs, 680 archbishops and bishops, 28 abbots, 29 generals of orders, in all 803. Besides important canons relating to the Faith and the constitution of the Church, the council decreed the infallibility of the pope when speaking *ex cathedra*, i.e. when as shepherd and teacher of all Christians, he defines

a doctrine concerning faith or morals to be held by the whole Church.

I think that most people would agree that memorable events in the history of the Church would have to include: the issues involved in the East-West Schism; the defection of Martin Luther; the decision to embark on the Crusades; the establishment of the Inquisitions; and the departure of the Anglicans.

However, no Ecumenical Council was convened to *specifically* address *any* of these events, although a couple were addressed in passing, albeit often long after the fact. Yet in retrospect, several of these Councils seemed to have had much more trivial agendas.

Rather than claim that "The Church has operated in the same way, by the same rules for 2,000 years and it has done just fine", the Institutional Church should acknowledge that it has endured by good fortune, acting pragmatically regarding necessary change and that this process must be refined so it operates with more alacrity, efficiency and transparency.

*****

Now let us consider the other pillar of Church proclaimed consistency, Canon Law. It is ironic in terms of the claim that "The Church has operated in the same way, by the same rules for 2,000 years and it has done just fine" that a major event in its development, occurring approximately at the halfway point in those 2,000 years was "The Gregorian Reform", which initiated the first attempts at a Code of Canon Law.

Father McBrien describes the Reform in *The Church*, this way (underlines are mine):

"The pontificate of Gregory VII (1073-85) and the so-called Gregorian reform, which he promoted so vigorously, have had profound and long-lasting effects on the exercise of papal authority and on the legalization of the papacy itself. When elected, Gregory confronted four interrelated challenges to the integrity of the Church: clerical corruption (including not only violations of celibacy, but also serious failures to attend to one's pastoral responsibilities), simony (the buying and selling of spiritual benefits, including church offices), nepotism (the promotion of one's relatives to high church offices), and lay investiture (the interference of temporal rulers in the internal life of the Church, especially with regard to the appointment and installation of bishops and abbots).

The Gregorian reform strengthened papal authority in its frequent disputes with temporal rulers, particularly Gregory's own bitter conflict with German Emperor Henry IV, and helped to free the Church from political domination. However, the reform, also tended to exaggerate the powers and the role of the papacy, declaring the Pope to be the supreme judge of all, including of bishops and abbots, with unlimited powers of absolution and excommunication and the right to depose emperors. Some of these claims were listed in the papal document *Dictatus Papae* (Lat., "Pronouncements of the Pope"), drafted (but never published) in March 1075. To establish a legal basis for such claims, Gregory encouraged the growth of a "cottage industry", canon law."

In other words, instead of power flowing from agreed upon law, the law was designed to fit and justify the assumed power. McBrien continues (again, underlines are mine):

"In the eleventh century there were concerted efforts to assemble older collections of ecclesiastical laws and regroup them according to the needs of the time. This led eventually to the formation of the new discipline of canon law, with its most famous collection Gratian's *Concordia Discordantium Canonum* (Lat., "Concordance of Discordant Canons"), also known simply as the *Decretum* ("Decree), which was completed by the famous Italian jurist around the year 1140. It became the standard textbook in Canon Law until the new Code of Canon Law appeared in 1917.

The *Decretum*'s topics included papal, conciliar and episcopal authority, various ministries, ordained and non-
ordained alike, the conditions of church membership, and
the sacraments."

Therefore, it appears that for the first eleven centuries of the Church there were some indeterminate
numbers of ecclesiastical laws in effect, described as
"discordant" or in at least some disagreement with one
another and of unknown provenance. These "collections" were refined and presumably integrated at the
request of a Pope to justify what he was already doing
and the result was a textbook on Canon Law, which
served the purpose of a juridical system for the next
nearly seven hundred eighty years.

It should be noted that the codification of Canon Law
was ordered by Vatican I in 1869. It took another forty-
eight years to produce it with, it should be noted no
input from those it was intended to govern. Obviously,
having an orderly set of guidelines, understood by the
average Catholic, has never been a high priority of the
Church.

Pope John XXIII, when announcing Vatican II in
1958 also announced that the Code of Canon Law would
be completely revised. That took until 1983. Since the
Executive, Legislative and Judicial powers of the Church
are reserved to the Pope, John's successors have been
unilaterally revising it many times, apparently to bring
it into line with what they want to do. However, this
concentration of power obviously weakens the Code in
the minds of many.

It should also be realized that Catholics in the pews
have been oblivious to all of these machinations. How
can I be sure of that? They must be or there would have
been a revolution. Yeah, right.

For people who live in democracies of various styles
around the world, the effectiveness of Legal Codes is
in direct proportion to the sincerity of the "consent of

the governed". Canon Law, with its disregard for the input of those who must live under it inspires few and its lack of explanation is accepted at face value by only the most Compliant and most of them are ignorant of what it contains.

Today's Code of Canon Law covers 1752 Canons in more than 8,000 pages and, by the way, the only "official" version is written in Latin. It is interesting to note that Mosaic Law contains only 613 Mitzvoth (commandments) promulgated over at least twice the period of time.

It is difficult to consider that "The Church has operated in the same way, by the same rules for 2,000 years and it has done just fine" is a sufficient justification for the maintenance of the status quo, in the face of the myriad problems confronting the Church.

The need for change is both obvious and imperative.

Chapter Five

The Conundrum of the Holy Spirit

I suspect that Psychologists studying early cognitive memory development of Catholic children from my era and perhaps later would find that "In the name of the Father, the Son and the Holy Ghost" was one of the first things installed there. It undoubtedly pre-dated the Pledge of Allegiance and the myriad other collections of words mostly meaningless to children at that age.

I could handle the concept of Father and Son, after all I had one and was another, but I really didn't understand the Holy Ghost and of course when it came to any questions about the Holy Trinity, the good Nuns and parish Priests all had the same four-word answer, "It is a mystery".

After I became an adult, perhaps when I saw Linda Blair's head swivel 360 degrees in *The Exorcist*, I decided that the Holy Ghost, by then called the Holy Spirit, was some kind of a Director of Special Effects for things like indoor winds before fans were invented, tongues of fire, burning bushes, parting seas and the like. I will admit that I did not have sufficient curiosity at that point to pursue the issue perhaps because I had accepted the premise that "it was a mystery" to which I was not yet privy. Besides, Google had not yet been developed.

Later, as I entered the computer age my metaphor changed again and I began to think of the Holy Spirit as God's e-mail system and easily assumed that there was: an "A-list", probably made up of the Pope, selected Cardinals and sage Theologians sequestered in monasteries; a "B-list" of hand-picked people like certain Bishops with Top Secret clearance and "need-to-know"; and beyond that several other less elite classifications, with people like me on the bottom tier, eligible only for innocuous mass mailings (pun thoughtfully intended) and ads for mansions in heaven.

Eventually, I began to get it. It *is* a mystery, but I was not searching for a deep Theological explanation with multiple scriptural references. I was looking for what a Theologian might tell his or her kids. Instead, I had to cobble together my own explanation. I had to find something to satisfy my curiosity to the point where I could think "well, it is something like that and since I am now sufficiently bored with the subject, I can get on with just believing it".

I'm not going to tell you what my explanation is because although it satisfies me, it might not satisfy you and I would be back at that boring task. We can probably all agree that there is *something* out there that explains *some* things like how people act and why *some* things happen, but let's leave it at that.

What I can and will tell you is that the times when I can't see evidence of the Holy Spirit successfully intervening with the operation of the Institutional Church are by far more troubling to me than when I am having a problem in my personal, professional or social life.

I understand the conflict between the Holy Spirit and human Free Will. Unlike what some of my Compliant Catholic friends contend about people like me, I do *not* believe that if I use my Free Will to do something that "makes it right, even if it isn't". Transgressions have consequences.

Some of the things contributing to my doubt or if you will my unbelief, have been and are:

- Why does it usually take several ballots to elect a Pope and why do they need a procedure that kicks in if they don't get enough votes after a set number of ballots? That should be a slam dunk. Are we to conclude that those who didn't vote for the "proper" (note that I did not say winning) candidate exercised their Free Will in *opposition* to the advice of the Holy Spirit? That would seem to me to be a pretty grievous sin.
- Why did it take the Church twenty some years to deal with Martin Luther's ninety-five objections and then to just say, "You are wrong. Goodbye", especially since in the centuries following the Church has embraced many of them?
- Why did it take over 450 years for the Church to decide it was not a good idea to have excommunicated Galileo for saying that the earth revolved around the sun and not vice versa, even though his claim was correct? The irony of this is that heliocentrism (the sun as the center of the universe, with earth and the other planets revolving around it) was developed much earlier by Copernicus. Galileo was censured, his writings were put on the Index and he was excommunicated for proving that theory, yet its author Copernicus, was never the object of any sanctions.
- Why is the Church always on the defense in creation versus evolution debates instead of being able to clearly articulate a position that simply accommodates the truth of both and ends the discussion?

- Why do the most important of the General Councils of the Church take so long and have such contentious debates? (Trent lasted eighteen years and Vatican I, which began in 1869 has never been officially closed)
- Why does the massive, secretive and opaque bureaucracy that is the Curia, always appear to be surprised at trends that seem so obvious to all of us? For example, how many incidents of clergy sexual abuse constitute a trend that should be addressed? I say one.
- In the same way, shouldn't someone have figured out fifty years ago that if a certain level of vocations were not maintained parishes would have to be closed?

Could it be that the Institutional Church thinks that the Holy Spirit is only in charge of carrying the messages they prepare to us, but isn't really involved in the development of those messages; or the elections of the Pope; or the actions of the Councils; or the administration of the Church? I am not alleging that, but don't you think that sometimes it appears that way.

Does any of this suggest that the Holy Spirit does not exist? Not at all. Does it suggest that the Holy Spirit is impotent? Of course not. The Holy Spirit is God. Does it suggest that the Holy Spirit should make all the decisions. Certainly not, we have enough Free Will to be occasionally stupid. Does it suggest that we or at least I just don't really understand the mission of the Holy Spirit? Perhaps.

Obviously that reasoning takes us back to those same four words: It is a mystery. Does that mean I disbelieve that "mystery"? No, only that my unbelief needs more explanation, but for the most part I am willing to wait on some of that until the afterlife, about which (as one would expect), I have a number of other questions.

Wouldn't a rational and helpful explanation be that we should all be open to the suggestions of the Holy Spirit on significant matters in our lives, but we shouldn't expect help for everything or answers for all of our questions? Sometimes we succeed or excel on our own and we should appreciate that. I don't believe that the Holy Spirit micromanages our lives, even if we pray for him or her to do that.

I think, in fact, the Holy Spirit probably receives credit for a lot of stuff she doesn't do or isn't, (like being male or female) and isn't recognized for many others, which are far more important. For example when I was writing the chapter which follows this one dealing with Vatican II, I had the following experience. This little story is completely true.

As I became immersed in the writing of that chapter, I began to feel that there was a simpler and more effective way to state the premise I was trying to develop. I decided to change the title of the chapter to "Blaming It All on Vatican II". Because it is the way I do things, I immediately scrolled back to the title and made the change.

As I was doing that, I was thinking I would need to do much more research on Vatican II than I had planned in order to make *that* case. Almost simultaneously, I received a signal that an e-mail had arrived. Since I am a bit compulsive about e-mail, I went to my Inbox.

The message was from Amazon saying that because of the content of some books I had previously purchased, they thought I might be interested in a book by John W. O'Malley, SJ, titled, *What Happened at Vatican II* and two others that were related. The books they mentioned I had purchased earlier turned out to be two I bought when I was doing research for *The Compliant, Curious and Critical Catholic* more than six years before.

Some of my less Critical Catholic friends have suggested to me that this was a case of the Holy Spirit operating on my behalf to help in writing this book. I am more inclined to believe that it is merely a testimony to the size and efficiency of the Amazon database, particularly because of the nature of my book. On the other hand, perhaps the Holy Spirit *wants* me to raise these issues and give you some things to think about regarding the state of the Church. I don't really know.

Nonetheless, I will admit that I <u>was</u> a bit curious about the timing of the e-mail. I bought all three books that were suggested and they have been extremely useful.

That said, I think that I need to be very clear on this point. My belief in the Trinity, including the Holy Spirit, her mission and her power, is unquestioned. With respect to my personal interaction with the Holy Spirit, I accept the possibility, even probability that some things that have happened to me have not been merely fortuitous coincidences and to the extent that they weren't I am very grateful.

Interaction with the Holy Spirit is just not something I expect on a daily basis or something that I would pray for except under conditions of extremis. That is perhaps a self-worthiness thing on my part.

In fact, when I have been confronted with a crisis or an apparently unsolvable dilemma, I don't pray that the problem will be just swept away or that a situation will be reversed, but that I will discover a way to deal with God's Will as it is.

You see, I believe that we come from God more or less completely equipped. I believe that He has given us what we need to deal with almost all of our problems. He actually has said as much. We just have to figure out where He put the proper tool. I even say a prayer of thanks for all the gifts God has given me, "even those that I haven't found yet". But that was another book.

Several years ago when I was in serious need of guidance about a number of things, I developed a practice I follow nearly every day. If I awake early and some time before I must get up, which happens quite frequently, I try to take advantage of that time by going through an exercise of ridding my mind of all urgent thoughts to the greatest extent possible.

If I am successful in doing that, I try to make myself open to whatever thoughts or ideas might be available. I accept them without being critical and allow them to take me where they will. This experience nearly always surprises me and often changes my life, albeit usually only slightly.

Some of those thoughts and ideas may in fact be the work of the Holy Spirit, but I don't really try to figure out which are and which are not. That, after all, would just be a self-serving waste of time. Some, perhaps most are probably *not* interventions by the Holy Spirit but I try to embrace them all, just in case.

I still wonder why the Holy Spirit would take the time to give me a hand with a book like this which is about informed dissent with the governance and discipline of the Church about which I am quite critical. However, perhaps giving me a hand on that subject is *exactly* why she intervened, although I certainly do not claim that. We will probably never know, but I still wonder.

Moreover, the interaction of the Holy Spirit with me or other individuals is not the conundrum referred to in the title of this chapter. That conundrum is in the relationship between the Holy Spirit and the leadership of the Institutional Roman Catholic Church, which is both real and totally obvious.

As a Catholic, Critical or otherwise it is difficult for me to conceive of anything more important to the Holy Spirit than the health, growth and well-being of the Catholic Church. In fact, that is what is claimed as the primary and perhaps sole mission of the Holy Spirit by many of the most vocal and fundamentalist thinking members of the hierarchy and their followers.

However, too often this is used as a rationale for the maintenance of the status quo, a position which begs the criticism of being contradictory. Moreover, since the Holy Spirit is God, for whom nothing is impossible, why has the Church been in steady decline for at least fifty years?

One could argue that the answer to that question is one of two logically obvious alternatives: Either those who hold the position that the growth, health and well being of the Roman Catholic Church are primarily important to the Holy Spirit are wrong; or those people are correct, but the Institutional Church leadership may not be open to the guidance of the Holy Spirit except as it relates to strengthening the status quo.

I challenge anyone to articulate a logical third alternative.

I do believe that the growth, health and well-being of the Church *are* of significant, if not primary interest to the Holy Spirit and therefore by definition God, so I categorically reject the first alternative.

Therefore, the only logical reason for the steady decline of the Catholic Church over at least the past fifty years is that many in the leadership of that Church *may not be open to* the guidance of the Holy Spirit except as it relates to strengthening the status quo. If that is the case, the intransigence goes back much farther than fifty years.

Of course, some might argue that the Holy Spirit is much more patient than we are and that change will come in time. I just don't accept that. The priority here is the preservation of the Church and the salvation of its members. That is not happening. I believe that the Holy Spirit is being ignored.

Ecclesiologists may think otherwise and correctly, but my uneducated guess is that this attitude has developed as a result of the proclamation of infallibility. For a little over a thousand years prior to Vatican I, the

Institutional Church was under *guidance* of the Holy Spirit, but the protection and governance of the Holy Roman Emperor. Many of the day to day rules were specified by the Emperor and therefore, many were more for the purpose of "good order and discipline" than any Theological reason.

When that comfortable alliance disappeared the Church was on its own to govern. Shortly, in historical contexts thereafter, the infallibility of the Pope was proclaimed.

Most of the faithful understand infallibility somewhat inaccurately. Clearly the Institutional Church obviously likes it that way and makes no attempt to enlighten them. So, with the faithful misunderstanding infallibility as they obviously do, who needs the Holy Spirit at least for temporal if not spiritual matters? It would appear that the Institutional Church hierarchy does not think *they* do and never did.

It should be noted that I am not asserting that the failure to be open to the guidance of the Holy Spirit has been an individual choice and willful act on the part of the succession of individual Popes and their advisors. Instead I believe that this is a systemic problem of oligarchies.

The leadership of the Institutional Church appears to believe that they may need Divine Guidance on matters of Faith and Morals, but when it comes to the Governance and Discipline of the structural Church and by extension the Laity, the leadership can handle it all by themselves, thank you very much. History appears to indicate that the Church is wrong in this regard, with the evidence being that the Church is falling apart before our eyes.

I am not asserting that the current Pope or any of his predecessors consciously closed their minds to the guidance of the Holy Spirit, although I am also not asserting that they didn't. I do assert that an *implied* extension of infallibility to the nameless and faceless Cardinals of the Curia has occurred. This *appearance of infallibility*, or "creeping infallibilism" (as Theologian Charles E. Curran describes it) then attached itself to virtually all documents and pronouncements emanating from the Vatican.

This phenomenon *may* have resulted in a systemic and institutional psyche by which they came to believe that the *counsel* of the Holy Spirit was *only* for matters of Faith and Morals. Then they *may* have concluded (appropriately in theory perhaps) that Governance and Discipline of the Institutional Church and the Laity was the exclusive purview of Curia Cardinals and the Pope. Therefore, the oligarchy no longer invites or heeds outside guidance, from the Holy Spirit or anyone else, much less the people affected.

This of course, is faulty reasoning on the part of the hierarchy.

Why should average Catholics, sitting in the pews of the parish church that now has only one Mass on the weekend because they share their Pastor with four other parishes, be surprised that their bishop won't listen to them, when the Holy Spirit can't get through to the Pope?

Let us look at the Institutional Church not from the point of view of the Theologians, but from that of the Catholic trying to get through this life in such a way as to make it into the next, better one, whatever that might be. After all, are we not told that we *are* the Church? Vatican II *declared* that, but John Paul II and Benedict XVI pretend we are not. While decrying temporal dictators, they behave just like them. Blessed my foot!

Most practicing Catholics (I admit that description could use some further definition, but it is used in its broadest possible sense) are not so much troubled by basic Theological dogmas. They are troubled by what they feel are arbitrary and often tenuous doctrinal extensions of those basic dogmas to the administrative rules *made by men* who govern Church members and their lives.

These are not like the arcane rules the Church has grudgingly changed with inordinate anguish, such as abstaining from meat on Fridays or on which Holy Days one must attend Mass, or currently the trivial struggle to agree on whether we should respond with "and also with you" or "and with your spirit" during Mass.

These are the bread and butter issues of the Catholic layperson's lives and include birth control, in-vitro fertilization, stem cell research, marriage and divorce.

They are also concerned about:

- Celibacy (as it affects the shortage of Priests)
- Attitudes about women and their place in the Church (which could be a partial solution as well)
- Reform of the Curia (which they correctly consider too doctrinaire, too secretive and too far out of touch)
- Collegiality (because they accurately believe that no one in the hierarchy listens to them or cares what they think).

It is both interesting and ironic to note that fifty years ago, during Vatican II most of those issues except marriage and divorce were on the agenda for discussion, but Pope Paul VI removed them from the table. One wonders where the Church might be today, had he not done that. One also wonders what the role of the Holy Spirit was *or was not* in that decision by the Pope.

I do not suggest that the hierarchy of the Church overtly *rejects* the guidance of the Holy Spirit when it comes to Governance and Discipline, but that it is not open to its consideration when it goes beyond basic dogma. I think that it is also fair to say that the Institutional Church has been aided and abetted in this position by Catholics who are Compliant, whose lack of intellectual curiosity makes them also complicit and to some degree culpably ignorant. They have let the hierarchy get away with this arrogant attitude for centuries.

As I have said earlier, I believe one might argue that this position on the part of the hierarchy goes back at least to just after the Civil War when it conferred on itself infallibility, which could in and of itself be considered the denial of the Holy Spirit. Remember, Pope Pius IX who declared himself infallible (assisted by those bishops who didn't flee rather than vote yes) also said, "I am tradition. I *am* the Church". I don't feel that the Church can have it both ways. However, I will leave that one to the Theologians.

Just as an aside, it seems inconceivable to me that after making that outrageous claim of personally being tradition *and* the Church, Pius IX was beatified on September 3, 2000! That is either outrageous or the sainthood process is questionable and certainly fallible.

The issue I am describing is more a practical one than a Theological one in nature. It is a matter of Governance and Discipline, not Faith and Morals. It is more related to practice than principle. It deals more with reality than the esoteric. And it goes far beyond that to an obsession for total power.

Catholics who are critical are outraged that the Institutional Church dismisses the worldwide problem of child abuse by Clergy as "idle gossip" and refuses to make public the documents containing information about the actions of the current Pope in such cases when he was an Archbishop in Germany. More relevant are his actions or lack of same when he was a Cardinal of the Curia, heading the Congregation for the Doctrine of the Faith which, ironically was formerly called the Supreme Sacred Congregation of the Roman and Universal Inquisition.

Catholics are incensed that those who preach about the need for personal responsibility for one's actions do not accept their own. Those who are Critical Catholics decry the fact that millions are dying of AIDS in Africa while the Institutional Church forbids the distribution and use of condoms, not for *birth* control but for *disease* control. In fact, the Church and its network of Dioceses and missionaries have a distribution system for condoms, which could vastly reduce the spread of AIDS within a generation.

It is as if the Institutional Church irrevocably decided in the middle of the nineteenth century that it knew all that there is to know about human nature and the world in which we all live and has refused to accept any further consideration of its position since that time. It has attempted to freeze us all in time.

The history of the Catholic Church for the past two thousand years shows it consistently to be reactive rather than proactive. It rarely anticipates problems and usually its reaction comes slowly. It took nearly a generation to react to the issues of Martin Luther. Then the reaction was arbitrary and ill-considered. Many of Luther's objections would not even be relevant today.

In a recent homily, my friend Father Bill O'Malley said, "If only the Catholics and Lutherans and Calvinists could have agreed Jesus was '*somehow*' more truly present in the Eucharist than anywhere else on earth, we'd all still be worshiping as one." Can that kind of damage be properly assessed?

*****

A reactive posture on the part of any organization or person generally reflects a lack of knowledge and as that thought entered my head I had a flashback to a phrase from a class in Moral Theology heard during my senior year at LeMoyne College in 1952, and taught by a memorable Jesuit, the Rev. Raymond J. H. Kennedy SJ. It was "Culpable Ignorance" which I found fascinating then and even more so now.

Not trusting my memory, I sent Google after confirmation and it came up with an article "Ignorance – Invincible and Vincible" by James Akin. It was originally published in *The Rock* magazine and I found it at CatholicCulture.org.

Here are the parts I found relevant to this chapter:

"In moral theology, ignorance is defined as a lack of knowledge that a person ought to have. Ignorance is distinguished from mere nescience, which is a lack of knowledge that a person has no need of. For example, a person who did not know the square root of 1429 would be ignorant of it if he were taking a math test, but he would be nescient of it if performing a task that didn't require the number.

Moral theology divides ignorance into a number of categories. The two I will consider here are *invincible* and *vincible*. Ignorance is invincible if a person could not remove it by applying reasonable diligence in determining the answer. Ignorance is vincible if a person *could* remove it by applying reasonable diligence. Reasonable diligence, in turn, is that diligence that a conscientious person would display in seeking the correct answer to a question given (a) the gravity of the question and (b) his particular resources.

The gravity of a question is determined by how great a need the person has to know the answer. The answers to fundamental questions (how to save one's soul, how to preserve one's life) have grave weight. The answers to minor questions (the solution to a crossword puzzle) have light weight.

The particular resources a person has include (a) the ease with which he can obtain the information necessary to determine the answer and (b) the ease with which he can make an accurate evaluation of the evidence once it is in his possession. The graver the question and the greater the resources available, the more diligence are needed to qualify as reasonable. The lighter the question and the fewer the resources available, the less diligence are needed to qualify as reasonable.

Just as it is possible to show less than reasonable diligence, it is also possible to show *more* than reasonable diligence. Diligence can be *supererogatory* (and praiseworthy) if one shows more diligence than would be expected from an ordinary, conscientious person. Diligence can be *excessive* or *scrupulous* (and blameworthy) if someone spends so much time seeking the answer to a particular question that he fails to attend to other matters he should attend to, or if he refuses to come to a conclusion and continues seeking even when he has enough evidence..."

Clearly, in this article Akin is referring to an individual's culpability for grave (mortal) sin. However, in the context of *this* book, I believe that the failure of the Institutional Church to thoroughly and as completely as possible *objectively* understand the world within which it operates institutionally, rises to that level.

In the same context, he goes on:

"If some, but insufficient, diligence was shown toward finding the answer, the ignorance is termed *merely* vincible. If little or no diligence was shown, the ignorance is termed *crass* or *supine*. If one deliberately fostered the ignorance then it is termed *affected* or *studied*.

If vincible ignorance is merely vincible, crass, or supine, it diminishes culpability for the sinful act relative to the degree of diligence that was shown. If a vincibly ignorant person showed *almost* reasonable diligence, most of his imputability for the sin could be removed. If he was crassly ignorant, having shown little or no diligence compared to what was reasonable, little or none of his imputability would be removed.

Affected or studied ignorance can increase culpability for a sin, especially if it displays hardness of heart, whereby one would commit the sin irrespective of any law that might exist concerning it. Such an attitude shows contempt for moral law and so increases culpability (cf. CCC 1859)...

In practical use, the terms *vincible* and *invincible* may pose problems for those unfamiliar with Catholic moral terminology. For many, *vincible* is a wholly unfamiliar term and *invincible* can suggest that which can *never* be overcome, no matter how much diligence is shown. Because of these difficulties, it may be advisable in practice to speak of *innocent* (invincible) and *culpable* (vincible) ignorance when addressing such people."

The key element in this argument is that the understanding postulated is objective. The Vatican operates actively in the diplomatic milieu and therefore undoubtedly collects vast amounts of information about the world. That does not assure that it is interpreted or applied objectively or even that it is accurate.

The gravity of the issue is obviously of extremely high weight. The diligence required is certainly *supererogatory*. The availability of the resources required is unquestioned.

So now the question is whether or not that ignorance of the world within which the Institutional Church operates, is *merely* vincible, or *crass* and or *studied*. I believe that if it is the result of not being open to the Holy Spirit except insofar as it relates to strengthening the status quo it is vincible, crass, studied and culpable ignorance.

We will never know for sure. However, for at least fifty years, successful corporations and most governments have had highly placed departments devoted to develop long term strategies for sustaining growth and well-being. They study demographic trends, technology forecasting and many other disciplines to minimize their impact.

Presumably, they do that without the assistance of the Holy Spirit. Just think of the advantage the Institutional Church would have with that kind of thinking _and_ the Holy Spirit! And while we are at it, why hasn't the hierarchy of the Institutional Church been *inspired* to do just that?

When I made that remark to a friend, he reminded me that during Vatican II Cardinal Seunens was inspired (perhaps by the Holy Spirit) to suggest the establishment of a *Secretariat for the Problems of the Contemporary World* as a department of the Curia. He wanted it to include laypersons.

And yet to many people the Church appears to have been stumbling along, historically reactive rather than proactive and there does not seem to be any discernable philosophical long-term strategy. This conundrum is obvious but is never discussed.

With or without the assistance of the Holy Spirit, the leadership of the Institutional Church should have taken the initiative long ago to be proactive in the development of a rational strategy on which to develop detailed plans. Has it not been irresponsible to ignore this reality?

Or are they just waiting for the Holy Spirit to show up with a completed plan? If so, that may be the epitome of both arrogance and presumption.

That same friend I just mentioned also has pointed out that "John Paul II and Benedict XVI have been so afraid of Communism and Materialism, which of course are not quite synonyms that they have looked back to what they consider the relative safety of the 19th Century. Ostriches are known for this behavior".

It seems to me that it is imperative for a detailed and coherent plan for the re-vitalization of the Church over the next fifty years to be developed and if the Holy Spirit shows up with some ideas and wants to help, so much the better. The default plan resulting from a failure to do that is to continue the current plunge to irrelevance, which is certain to take much less than fifty years.

There is no doubt that some among you are disturbed by my assumption that no such clear strategy and supporting plans are currently in place. Good point. However, if they are in place, they are not visible, they are not working and something needs to be done about that.

The apparent strategic objective of the Institutional Church for the foreseeable future is to assure that the status quo is preserved and strengthened, regardless of the consequences. This of course is based on the myth that "the Church has operated the same way for 2000 years without change and it will for another 2000 years". I can only hope that the previous chapter dealing with that myth helped to put it to rest.

I certainly cannot presume to suggest a definitive strategic objective and plan for the Church and that is not the purpose of this book. I can however guarantee that to survive, one is needed and it must be articulated clearly and unambiguously to every Catholic in the world. Only then can supporting plans be developed to assure that the objective is achieved. It may take Vatican III.

Ironically, the clear acceptance and support of such a plan by the people in the pews are essential to its success. That reality may very well make it a document, which cannot be written.

That is not to say that the plans supporting the objectives of the strategy would *necessarily* include a married clergy, or a change in the birth control policy, or a stronger place for women in the Church, or a more humane process for dealing with bad marriages, or a real collegial structure that works, or a plan for eliminating child abuse, or an effective plan to eliminate poverty, or a plan for any other ill afflicting the Church and its people. But these possibilities must be considered in the context of charity and reality, rather than merely a knee-jerk reaction.

In this process, there is the possibility of an objective re-evaluation of the man made and therefore fallible and outdated doctrines, edicts, practices and procedures, which have crept into the institutional church.

However, almost by definition, the responsibility for satisfying that possibility lies squarely within the confines of Vatican City.

Would this process drive some people out of the Church? Probably. Would it help retain some of the Catholics who are critical? Certainly. Would it bring back some who have left? Perhaps, if they believe the new plans are real. Is it risky? You're damned right!

Is the alternative riskier? Just look around.

Chapter Six

Myth Two: Blame It All On Vatican II

F ew Catholics could tell you the years in which Vatican II was convened. However, many Catholics are convinced that the majority of the problems of the Catholic Church are the result of it. That much is something about which some Compliant and some Critical Catholics seem to totally agree, but they really do not.

Those who are *critical* think the Council didn't go far enough in addressing the problems facing the Church and that the modest gains which it did make have been subverted by the successor Popes. Those who are *compliant* believe the Council went much too far, but they often don't know how or why. This anomaly in the view of those compliant Catholics who think that the Council went too far is the result of being either uninformed or misinformed.

Obviously, during the twenty centuries since Christ the world has become a very different place for a variety of reasons. Human knowledge and understanding have developed almost immeasurably. We no longer believe the world is flat or that it is the center of the Universe. Population has skyrocketed. We have discovered there were entire civilizations, which had flourished in obscurity, before and during the time of Christ.

In the past hundred years the growth of technology has expanded beyond anyone's imagination. Infinitely more things are possible today than ever before and more are on the way.

However, that certainly does not mean that the basic articles of our Faith have been rendered obsolete. Nor does it mean that basic Moral standards have either. Moreover, there are many more things to which those standards must be applied and many new conditions which make such applications difficult, if not impossible without modification.

That is just the way it is. If Christ were to return today, He would be faced with far different situations and would have to adapt in order to address them. He would do that. That does not mean that he would be contradicting himself.

For the better part of 2,000 years (a relatively small percentage of the history of human kind) Catholics have relied on their leaders because those leaders were more educated and more powerful, to define that basic Faith and those Moral principles. However, that is no longer the case. Ordinary Catholics are now often better educated than their leaders. Unfortunately, those leaders usually will not listen to them.

For at least three quarters of the history of the Church, Popes made many decisions and proclamations which, because of the primitive level of communications at the time most Catholics never heard about, never accepted and never really cared.

Then came the Protestant Reformation sparked by Martin Luther's publication of his ninety-five theses in 1517. This sparked a not so prompt reaction in the form of the Council of Trent (1545-1563) to formalize dogma and doctrines regarding Faith and Morals. A prominent role in that formalization of doctrine was played by the first Congregation of the Curia to be established, the Congregation of the Inquisition, now called the Congregation for the Doctrine of the Faith.

Following the first Vatican Council in 1869-1870, the Institutional Church became far more dogmatic and less willing to accept change. This is the way that today's Compliant Catholics believe the Church has *always* been and the way they want it to remain.

This formalization was furthered during Vatican I when it was decreed that a Code of Canon Law was to be developed. However, it took fifty years to complete it before its promulgation in 1917. Forty years later, in announcing Vatican II, Pope John XXIII also announced that the Code was to be completely revised. More will be said about Canon Law in a later chapter.

The reasons for this disconnect between the Compliant and Critical Catholic reactions to Vatican II is that pretty much by definition Compliant Catholics are not receptive to change and they often are not curious enough to educate themselves about things which make them uncomfortable. When it comes to Vatican II, they assume that "the Liberals", whoever they were, somehow slipped some things past the Council when no one was paying attention and that annoys them. They are not certain what those things were, but they are convinced that they don't like them.

I have tried to understand what the term "Liberals", as used by Compliant Catholics really means and with great difficulty I am beginning to do so. The closest I can get to that meaning is: A "Liberal" Catholic is anyone who accepts a rational need for change regardless of how insignificant in the teaching, practice, ritual, music or architecture of the Institutional Church.

Curious and Critical Catholics are by definition more attuned to and knowledgeable about their religion, its history and the resultant logical need for occasional change. They are inaccurately labeled "Liberal", which is really much more a political term than an ecclesiological description.

By exclusion then, a Conservative (Compliant) Catholic is one who rejects *any* change in the teaching, practice, ritual, music or architecture, which he or she believes have occurred since the time of Christ. The problem is that they do not realize how absurd that position really is.

These well-meaning Compliant Catholics take the position that the Church did very well believing and doing things exactly the same way for nearly two thousand years, but since Vatican II everything has gone downhill. I suppose if they believe that Pope Alexander VI was a model of Christian living, that the Crusades were a great idea, that the failure to consider the grievances of Martin Luther was a wise decision, that Galileo deserved excommunication, that the Inquisition was moral, that the Index furthered human knowledge and that ignoring the Holocaust merits sainthood, then they might have a point.

They probably also don't realize that as recently as 1917, one could be a Cardinal without being a Priest.

I think I have demonstrated that the prior two thousand were not without significant change, albeit some good and some bad.

Over the past several years I have heard the following allegations of things that were direct or indirect results of Vatican II: statues had to be removed from the churches; Catholics were instructed to not pray the Rosary as much as before; all veneration of the Virgin Mary was to be downplayed; one's conscience was declared to be whatever you want it to be and nothing is sinful, unless you think it is.

While I was writing this chapter, I went to the funeral of a friend of more than forty-five years and ran into another friend of equal duration. He kidded me about being an author and implied that he had read my first book.

I asked how he was doing and he said, "I'm coping". I laughed and told him that I was writing a new book called "The Coping Catholic" (that was the working title at the time). He said that was a great title because since Vatican II (which was going on when I first met him) coping is about the only thing a Catholic can do these days. He went on to say, "they took all the statues out, now they are taking out the candles. I walk into a church these days and can't tell if it is Catholic or not. I guess in the end, the Protestants won". I decided that he probably didn't read my first book after all and certainly will not like this one. I told him that he would love my new book. I didn't tell him he was going to be quoted in it.

The fact of the matter is that Vatican II did none of these things my friend mentioned. All of this is hyperbole, malicious or otherwise from people who have not taken the time to seek the truth.

The great irony here is that most of the *Critical* Catholics with whom I have talked feel that Vatican II was largely a failure because it did not do enough, what it did do was not pursued with sufficient vigor and that most of it has been rolled back, by a reactionary Institutional Church. In fact they feel that virtually all that remains of the impact of Vatican II is that Mass is said in the language of the country; the altar was turned around; women are sometimes treated marginally better; the Index that had been a joke among scholars for centuries disappeared; the music got better; and we can eat meat on Friday.

Vatican II was announced by Pope John XXIII, on January 25, 1959, nearly fifty-one years to the day before I first wrote this page. It was in session from October 1962 until December 1965, with the actual deliberations being in session during the last three or four months of each of those years. In between there was a great deal of research, drafting and re-drafting of positions and old-fashioned lobbying going on. Since there was no cable news in those days, many people including me weren't really following its progress or lack of same even on a yearly basis.

I am one of those no-name generation "tweeners" living in semi-obscurity between The Greatest Generation and the Baby Boomers. We grew up in "the old Church", embraced the concept of Vatican II and now sometimes wonder, "What the hell was that all about?" Many of those who came before us didn't much accept Vatican II and those who came after us didn't much care.

When I first heard about Vatican II, it sounded like a good idea, but that was the extent of my thinking about it because I didn't see how it would affect me one way or another. That was a busy time in my life. We had three young children and during that period I made a major job change, moved to a new city and built a new house. I was far more interested in ridding my lawn of crab grass than in following the deliberations of a basilica full of bishops speaking Latin, thousands of miles away.

Ironically, after I began writing this chapter, I became aware of a book called *What Happened At Vatican II*, written by noted Historian and Theologian John W. O'Malley, SJ and published by the Harvard University Press. The circumstances of my learning about this book were described in the previous chapter.

When I read it I was reminded of more things about Vatican II than I thought I knew and I learned about a number of other things that I wish I had known before. They would have been useful in a number of discussions I have been in with my Compliant Catholic friends. Moreover, I didn't find anything to substantiate any of the allegations I had heard them make.

Suddenly I realized that a great deal of the "folk lore" both positive and negative depending on your point of view, which has developed about Vatican II is just not true. Therefore, it seemed to me that a clarification of Vatican II is an essential chapter in a book about coping Catholics. The O'Malley book has been very helpful in this regard.

The fact is that most Catholics did not have a clear idea of what was going on during Vatican II when it was happening, and in the years since, they have forgotten what little they did know. Some actually consider it to have been some sort of a Papal coup engineered by "a few of *those Liberals* who have ruined the Church".

John XXIII did not convene Vatican II to ruin or even revolutionize the Church. To use his word, he sought "aggiornamento", an Italian word for update based on the conditions of the day.

Furthermore, the facts are that the rules and procedures under which Vatican II operated were heavily stacked against any change at all. Let us look at the process that was used, as described by Father O'Malley, so that you can determine for yourself whether a coup was involved.

In June of 1959, 2,598 Bishops and Prelates from around the world were asked to suggest all of the issues needing action that he thought should be addressed and resolved. A total of 1,998 (77%) of them submitted lists of issues to be considered.

O'Malley provides us a list of some of the issues most frequently mentioned:

- The use of the organ in church services.
- The place of Aquinas in the curriculum of seminaries.
- The legitimacy of stockpiling nuclear weapons.
- The blessing of water used for Baptism.
- The role of the laity in church ministries.
- The relationship of the bishops to the Pope.
- The purpose of marriage.
- Priests salaries.

- The role of conscience in moral decision making.
- Proper clothing for nuns.
- The Church's relationship with the Arts.
- Marriage among deacons (!?).
- Translation of the Bible.
- Boundaries of dioceses
- Legitimacy or illegitimacy of worshipping with non-Catholics.

And there were many others.

This provides an interesting, if not disturbing insight into the episcopal mind, but is hardly the stuff of revolution.

In addition, each of the thirteen Congregations of the Roman Curia (there is a fourteenth Congregation, but its purview is the Eastern Rite Churches) was asked to provide their issues and that produced another 400 pages of suggestions. However, Father O'Malley reports that "By and large (these latter) responses called for a tightening of the status quo; for condemnations of modern evils whether inside the Church or outside; and for further definitions of doctrines, especially those relating to the Virgin Mary".

Father O'Malley goes on to enumerate the issues that were the most important at the Council, saying, "the desire to recognize the dignity of lay men and women and to empower them to fulfill their vocation in the Church was certainly among them". (It should be noted that this issue was met with the least opposition in the Council and easily agreed upon.) However, it has turned out that this was largely lip service, since if anything the Institutional Church has ignored the voice of the laity with even greater vigor and regularity.

That does not mean that the Council was merely a "rubber stamp" for the Vatican. In fact, the opposition was well represented and not timid in their response.

O'Malley also said:

"Generally speaking, the most important issues were the most hotly contested. This almost invariably meant that some bishops rightly or wrongly perceived them as deviating from previous practice or teaching to such an extent as to be dangerous, or illegitimate, or heretical. The amount of time the Council spent in dealing with an issue, whether on the floor of the Council or in meeting in other venues, signaled the importance attached to it. The time spent was often in direct proportion to the degree to which the issue seemed to violate received teaching or practice.

Three issues were in this regard so sensitive or potentially explosive that Pope Paul withheld them from the Council's agenda—clerical celibacy, birth control, and the reform of the Roman Curia (the central offices of the Vatican). To these must be added the Synod of Bishops, which Pope Paul created during Vatican II without having made any provision for the council to act on the measure or participate in its formation. These four issues, supposedly not issues *of* the council, were nonetheless issues *at* the council, and thus are important for understanding what happened."

In Father O'Malley's opinion the remaining key issues, which were addressed by the Council were and their rationales were:

- "...The place of Latin in the liturgy...This issue, important in its own right, also had deeper ramifications. It was a first awkward wrestling with the question of the larger direction the council should take—confirm the status quo or move notably beyond it".
- "The relationship of Tradition to Scripture...Underneath the contention on this seemingly technical theological question lurked questions of wider significance—first, the prescriptive value of earlier doctrinal statements (in this instance, the decree of the Council of Trent on this subject), and second, the way the teaching authority of the Church relates to Scripture. Closely associated with the Scripture-Tradition question, moreover, was the question of how far modern methods of literary and historical interpretation were legitimate as applied to the Bible."
- "Few issues ignited such bitter controversy both inside and outside the council as the relationship of the church to the Jews, and then to other non-Christian religions... The relationship of the Catholic Church to other Christian

churches also had a rough ride, but not nearly so rough as the relationship to the Jews. The latter was particularly difficult partly because of its potentially political implications in the Arab world, and partly because of the negative statements 'about Jews' in the New Testament. John's gospel, for instance, consistently describes 'the Jews' as Jesus' enemies."

- "The declaration On Religious Liberty traveled a similarly difficult path. Its advocacy of forms of separation of church and state, as well as a kind of primacy it gave to conscience over obedience to ecclesiastical authority, aroused fierce opposition, which threatened...(its) viability."

- "The document 'On the Church in the Modern World'... sparked controversy of a different kind, not only because of some of the particular issues it addressed, such as the stockpiling of nuclear weapons and the aims of marriage (with its implication for birth control), but also because of its sprawling scope, its lack of precedent in any previous council, a tone some judged too optimistic, and the sociological or empirical approach it sometimes seemed to be basing itself upon."

"Although the...document (On the Church) met criticism on many points and was revised accordingly, none of its provisions turned out to be more contentious and more central to the council's agenda than the relationship of the bishops, or the episcopal hierarchy, to the papacy. The technical expression for the relationship the council advocated was "collegiality". What kind of authority did the bishops have over the church at large when they acted collectively, that is collegially; how was that authority exercised in relationship to the pope; and how was collegiality different from "Conciliarism' (supremacy of council over pope), a position condemned in the fifteenth century and repeatedly condemned thereafter?"

O'Malley goes on to say (underlines are mine):

"As the council hammered out the positions that eventually prevailed on these issues, it was carried along by an overwhelmingly large majority of bishops. Nonetheless, <u>a small minority—10 to 15 percent—adamantly opposed</u> the trends and made their influence felt in many ways. Tempers flared. Harsh words were exchanged, accusations made. The leaders of the minority emerged early and remained constant...This struggle between the majority and the minority, so easy to oversimplify, constitutes an essential component of the history of Vatican II..."

However, eighty-five to ninety percent in the majority hardly describes a coup, does it?

In summary of this subject, Father O'Malley says:

"...at Vatican II there were 'issues under the issues' at work. He says, "I believe there were at least three: (1) the circumstances under which change in the church is appropriate and the arguments with which it can be justified; (2) the relationship in the church between center and periphery, or, to put it more concretely, how authority is properly distributed between the papacy, including the Congregations (departments or bureaus) of the Vatican Curia, and the rest of the church; and (3) the style or model according to which that authority should be exercised"...

"These issues are key to understanding Vatican II. They are, moreover, critically important for anyone who is interested in grasping the tensions and conflicts within the Catholic Church today. In their abstract formulation these topics sound perennial, yet in their concrete manifestations they are current and urgent".

Now we are getting to the heart of the matter, the controversy about Vatican II and the problems in the Church today. Those issues have still not been addressed. In fact, they have been systematically ignored.

We will now return to the *process* of Vatican II. All of the selected issues were sorted, consolidated where possible and then each was assigned to one of the ten Preparatory Commissions, which had been set up by the Pope. Each of these Commissions was chaired by the head of one of the Congregations of the Curia.

The Curia, of course is the administrative and religious bureaucracy that surrounds the Pope and it includes the thirteen Congregations, each of which is responsible for a specific Theological aspect of the

Church. The concept first appeared in a document written by Pope Urban II in 1089. However, the first Congregation was not founded until 1584 under Pope Paul III. So, for nearly eighty percent of the history of the Church, the Congregations of the Curia did not exist.

Ironically as was mentioned earlier, although the Curia itself was one of the issues of Vatican II, this was largely finessed by Paul VI who said he would deal with it outside the Council, but he lacked the courage to undertake it. An editor might argue that I understate this observation.

The job of the Preparatory Commissions was to develop a number of Schemas, or position papers from the Curia; to specify those issues to be debated; and to determine how they would then to be voted upon by nearly 2,900 members of the Council. In other words, the custodians of the status quo decided the issues to be discussed; set the official starting positions on them; defined the manner in which they could be modified; and specified the size of the majority required to adopt the final version. No opportunity for a coup there.

Fortunately, that was not the end of the process. When the Council opened, the voting members elected from their peers members of each Council Commissions who were organized on a one for one basis as the Preparatory Commissions. These new Commissions were to present the Schemas, conduct the debate and take the votes.

To further stack the deck against change, the heads of the Preparatory Commissions all moved to the Council Commissions although they were joined by fifteen others from the Council at large. Recognizing what had been done, Pope John then added more members to each Commission to assure broad representation.

During the debate on a Schema, only a simple majority was needed to send the document back to the Commission with recommendations for revision. There

115

was effectively no limit to the number of times a Schema could be returned for revision.

Since no matter how minor, these Schemas represented changes in the status quo and a higher standard was set for passage of the final document. That standard was two-thirds, ironically the same formula the US Senate requires to end filibusters. As a practical matter, *only one of the final Schemas came close to be defeated* and still garnered more than seventy percent of the votes. Most of the rest were passed by around ninety percent. The majority had spoken loudly.

Initially, there were sixteen Schemas to be presented. That was expanded to seventeen, but as time went on, there was some consolidation and the final number was thirteen.

Nonetheless, from the outset the deck was *clearly stacked against* any significant change.

Two Popes were involved with Vatican II, its sponsor John XXIII and after just one session his successor Paul VI. Their approaches were quite different. John was content, even enthusiastic that the Council would work through the task on its own terms. Unfortunately, he lived through only the first of the Council's four years.

Pope Paul on the other hand was a micro-manager, inserting himself into the debate and working behind the scenes. He never seemed very enthusiastic about the whole concept. Some might even deduce that he hoped it would fail.

Of course, there is the usual array of conspiracy theories, but I do not consider them to be suitable matters for inclusion in this book. I will leave them to authors more interested in developing screenplays than in getting to the truth.

However, for those hoping for the change John had promised, Pope Paul acted most egregiously when he took three key issues completely off the table (Celibacy, Birth Control and Reform of the Curia) and he significantly limited any meaningful debate and action on Collegiality, by doing an end run on the issue and establishing an essentially impotent Synod of Bishops. The negative consequences of those actions seriously affect the Church today, forty-five years later.

The late Father Francis X. Murphy, a Redemptorist Theologian was appointed as a Peritus to the Redemptorist Bishop Aloysius Willinger of the Diocese of Monterey-Fresno, California during Vatican II. Periti were expert Theologians assigned to assist each Bishop attending the Council, but Murphy added another private and personal task to that assignment. Writing under the pseudonym of Xavier Rynne, Murphy published a series of comprehensive articles in *The New Yorker* about the Council, during the four years it was happening. Recently, these articles were collected and published in book form as *Vatican II* by Orbis Books.

Father Murphy's book and *What Happened at Vatican II*, by John W. O'Malley, SJ provide two non-redundant insights to the Council. They are worthwhile reading for any Catholic, compliant, curious, critical or otherwise.

Most informed Catholics would probably agree that the long-term impact on their lives from Vatican II has been little beyond the changes I mentioned earlier: "Mass is said in the language of the country; the altar was turned around; women are sometimes treated marginally better; the Index that had been a joke among scholars for centuries essentially disappeared; the music improved a little; and we can eat meat on Friday".

And what about the allegations about those things that were direct or indirect results of Vatican II: statues had to be removed from the churches; Catholics were instructed to not pray the Rosary as much as before; all veneration of the Virgin Mary was to be downplayed; one's conscience was declared to be whatever you want it to be and nothing is sinful, unless you think it is?

Statues: The second Vatican Council stated that the placement of statues in churches should be continued. However, it suggested that common sense be used regarding the quality and suitability of those statues. The Council never intended for an elimination of all statues or even a trend toward minimalism. For example, some churches because of their size or traditional style can and should have considerably more statutes than a contemporary or small church.

"The practice of placing sacred images in churches so that they may be venerated by the faithful is to be maintained. Nevertheless their number should be moderate and their relative positions should reflect right order, for otherwise they may create confusion among the Christian people and foster devotion of doubtful orthodoxy." *Sacrosanctum Concilium 125*

"...Ordinaries must be very careful to see that sacred furnishings and works of value are not disposed of or dispersed; for they are the ornaments of the house of God." *Sacrosanctum Concilium 126*

The Rosary: The Rosary was not specifically mentioned in Vatican II, although there was certainly no intention to eliminate this popular prayer. I could find no source for this incorrect interpretation of Vatican II. However, some priests and bishops recognizing the emphasis the Council placed on the Eucharist have tried to reduce the misguided practice of praying the rosary throughout the celebration of Mass. Good for them, I say. Each thing in its proper place.

Veneration of Mary Should Be Downplayed: Likewise, this was not discussed. However, it is true that some proposals were made for Mary to be accorded an even more prominent position than has been traditional. The vast majority of the Council voted to not consider those proposals because it was felt that they suggested parity of the Virgin Mother with the Holy Trinity.

In any case, there was no suggestion that then current veneration be reduced.

Conscience: Vatican II reaffirmed that one's conscience is the exercise of one's responsibility in using Free Will. In no way did it allow us to make up our own rules. Some people just cannot handle that responsibility and so they either did nothing or sought out the most rigid positions to follow. Vatican II placed the responsibility squarely where it belongs, on the individual concerned. It made us responsible for searching out the facts about a situation, making a logical and correct judgment about a course of action and accepting the result.

It was not a license to sin.

However, I believe that in failing to address the most critical issues of the time, i.e. birth control, celibacy, reform of the Curia and collegiality, Vatican II did not go far enough and failed in the mission John XXIII set for it. This was an opportunity lost. This is the root cause of the situation we have today with a disillusioned laity, a struggling clergy, impotent bishops (most of them recommended by the Restorationist Cardinal Ratzinger and 80% appointed by John Paul II) and a hierarchy serving its own self-interest instead of the church of Christ.

Chapter Seven

The After Myth:
The Restoration

T he Sixties was arguably the most transforming
decade in American history and perhaps the most
definitive cultural change in the history of the world. It
was crammed with events, good and bad which collectively contributed to that revolution of thinking.

For example (in no particular order and an incom-
plete collection): introduction of "the pill" and the sexual
revolution; the assassinations of President Kennedy,
Medgar Evers, Martin Luther King, Jr., Malcom X,
George Lincoln Rockwell and Robert Kennedy; the laser;
construction of the Berlin Wall; the emergence of the
Internet; the Cuban Crisis; Hurricane Camille; the Viet
Nam War; the first heart transplant; the Bay of Pigs
disaster; women's liberation; the Civil Rights Struggle;
the Six Day War between Israel on one side and Egypt,
Jordan, Syria, Iraq, Saudi Arabia, Sudan, Tunisia,
Morocco and Algeria on the other, with Israel the quick
victor; the Watts Riots; the Gulf of Tonkin incident and
the forfeiture by the Congress of its Constitutional right
to determine when and with whom we go to war; organization of NOW; the "I have a dream" speech; Woodstock,
which celebrated the counter cultural lifestyle; the social

revolution; nuclear proliferation; Betty Friedan and *"The Feminine Mystique"*; the Manson Murders; establishment of Miranda Rights; Nelson Mandela sentenced to life in prison; the mini skirt and the bikini; "Mississippi Burning"; the Beatles; the Gay Rights Movement; the Tet Offensive; Jane Fonda; the Cold War; the discontinuation of the Motion Picture Association of America's Production Code; the Kent State Massacre; Timothy Leary and the "Turn on, tune in, drop out" drug culture; the general fall from grace of many institutions including the Church, civil authority, the military, universities and the government; the revolt spreading to challenge authority of any kind; the Apollo I fire; a man walked on the moon, to name a few.

And Vatican II.

At the same time, the Catholic Church in America was losing priests, nuns and ordinary laymen in record numbers. Vatican II has been blamed for that exodus by both those who had hoped the Council would make significant changes and by those who said that too many changes had been made. Does that mean that if Vatican II had never been convened, no one would have left?

I doubt it. I believe that those numbers would have been much larger. The innate optimism of many Catholics fostered the development of a false hope that Vatican II had been a start and that meaningful change in the future was possible. This was a miscalculation of historic proportions.

Candidly, there was so much going on in the Sixties that it is doubtful that many Catholics were paying much attention to the day to day deliberations among 3,000 or so bishops in Vatican City. The undeniable disconnect between the hierarchy and the rest of the Church had long been established. Ordinary Catholics were used to the "Do what we say and keep your mouth shut" treatment and if they thought about it at all, they were probably hoping that the new stuff would just not be a greater burden than the old. The same old story of "pray, pay and obey".

Certainly some priests and religious left for each of those allegations about the Council. It is also likely that some left just because others did and no doubt at least some found Vatican II a convenient excuse to make the break without having to explain their real reasons. Not to be overly cynical about it, but for some young men who turned eighteen from 1941 through 1945 or so and entered the seminary rather than to go to war, it may have just been a mid-life crisis thing.

That said it is difficult to ignore that Paul VI made the decision to not allow the Council to even discuss birth control, celibacy and collegiality as promised by John XXIII and that was in itself a strong message to all from and about the Institutional Church. They had made it crystal clear that substantive changes in the things most important to those in the pews and the pulpit were going to be increasingly more difficult to achieve, just in case anyone dared to think otherwise.

The simple message that change was not an option was a more powerful incentive for departure than any possible combination of individual issues. However, there were many other longer term reasons for the decline in Church membership.

I would venture to guess, that if all the priests who stayed had known what they were in for and what the Church is today, the Exodus would have been even larger. A current pastor who I have known for quite a while, avers that Vatican II was the *least* relevant cause for the defection of priests, nuns and ordinary laymen from the Church. The problem is in the Institutional Church.

*****

Ironically, prior to Vatican II the Institutional Church was just beginning to welcome as active adults a much higher percentage of college educated people than ever before and that trend has continued. Unfortunately for the Church, but fortunately for the people that education prompted and developed a desire to make one's own informed decisions about things affecting them, including the Church. Such decisions involved obtaining information and applying reason and logic in a coherent process.

However, the Institutional Church seemed to insist upon a further test of conscience with the caveat that the application of conscience is *only* valid if it fully conforms to *their* established position. That circular reasoning flew in the face of their education. Moreover, there had been no debate about this by the *real* Church and therefore no specific guidance. Since Vatican I and the declaration of infallibility, the ultimate priority of the Institutional Church had always been just the maintenance of the status quo, until the promise of John XXIII.

The people had many incentives to leave during the sixties and they indeed still do today. Sadly, the Institutional Church didn't then and does not now provide any real incentives to stay other than "if you leave you are headed for Hell". Instead they offer "involvement" and "community", which far too often mean "pious busy work" and forced "sociability" in order to elicit loyalty.

Magisterium was reduced to a requirement that Homilies must explain the scripture readings, but many priests and deacons are not prepared or even capable of that task. Instead they merely repeated the passages with an internal commentary. This practice continues to the present, while, the morality of major issues like immigration, gun control, health care and poverty are ignored or left untouched.

Just as an aside for example, how many people do you suppose understand the Church's position on Gun

Control and specifically private gun ownership? This is an excerpt of an article from The Catholic News Service, written by Carol Glatz and published January 14, 2011:

> VATICAN CITY (CNS) — The Catholic Church's position on gun control is not easy to find; there are dozens of speeches and talks and a few documents that call for much tighter regulation of the global arms trade, but what about private gun ownership?
>
> The answer is resoundingly clear: Firearms in the hands of civilians should be strictly limited and eventually completely eliminated.
>
> But you won't find that statement in a headline or a document subheading. It's almost hidden in a footnote in a document on crime by the U.S. bishops' conference and it's mentioned in passing in dozens of official Vatican texts on the global arms trade.
>
> The most direct statement comes in the bishops' "Responsibility, Rehabilitation and Restoration: A Catholic Perspective on Crime and Criminal Justice" from November 2000.
>
> "As bishops, we support measures that control the sale and use of firearms and make them safer — especially efforts that prevent their unsupervised use by children or anyone other than the owner — and we reiterate our call for sensible regulation of handguns."
>
> That's followed by a footnote that states: "However, we believe that in the long run and with few exceptions — i.e. police officers, military use — handguns should be eliminated from our society."

Regardless of your own personal position on this matter and, in the interest of full disclosure I support the position as stated, don't you think that should have been the topic of a Homily, even back in November 2000 when the USCCB announced it? Or just after the shooting of Congresswoman Gabrielle Giffords in Tucson? Or any other such national event? Or try, "just because they should".

Would it not be refreshing and creative if some homilist somewhere tied the story of Peter relieving that guy of his ear to "early sword control"?

Just out of curiosity, I wonder if any bishops are withholding communion from National Rifle Association members. I mean, fair is fair.

Post Vatican II recognition of the value of women to the Institutional Church has often amounted to allowing them to find seats for the parishioners in half-empty churches and trusting them take up the collection. Collegiality was given lip-service by the creation of Parish Councils, which all too often ended up being rubber stamps for the Pastor who has always had his own cadre of informal advisors.

Since few Catholics today really believe that outside the Church there is no salvation, the reaction to Vatican II was that some just left and many others just gritted their teeth, ignore the things with which they disagree and cope.

In the 2012 Presidential nominating season, one of the front-running candidates is a man who abandoned Catholicism and joined the Lutheran Church when he married. That was in 1988 and certainly not because of Vatican II. He and his wife are now Evangelical Baptists, a sect that is known for its strong disgust for Catholicism. It will be interesting how compliant Catholics and especially Catholics who have left the Church but not affiliated with another denomination will react to him.

There is no doubt that Vatican II contributed to the exodus of Catholics from the Church during the late sixties and early seventies, but it was not a significant contribution. Other causes were many and varied. I suspect that often Vatican II was a more comfortable excuse than the truth would have been. Moreover that was a one-time loss and does not explain the situation today.

Those who left the Church for whatever reason damaged the Church that existed up until 1975 in terms of its population, but little else and have done little or no damage since. The inexorable collapse of the Church since 1975 is not the fault of those who left, but those who stayed.

Two generations of Catholics who stayed have reached maturity since that time. Any person who was 21 or older when Vatican II ended is on Social Security. Any person who was born the year Vatican II closed was forty-five years old in 2010. Any priest who was ordained before Vatican II is at least seventy years old now. The youngest bishop in the United States as I write this was born in 1966, the year after Vatican II closed.

Those who left did not cause the problems we face today and they almost surely could not have fixed them if they had stayed.

Vatican II wasn't responsible for the sexual abuse scandal or its cover-up. Vatican II is not the reason that the Institutional Church can't figure out how to increase vocations to the priesthood. Vatican II is not the reason that Catholic Schools are closing or that parishes are being consolidated. Vatican II is not responsible for the Institutional Church losing its credibility and its voice in the public square.

Vatican II isn't responsible for the state of the Institutional Church today because Pope John Paul II, under the guidance, if not control, of Cardinal Ratzinger now Benedict XVI virtually dismantled it and now seems intent on taking us back to Vatican I.

As the illustrious philosopher Pogo once wisely said, "We has met the enemy and they is us".

The Institutional Church is what it is today because of a monumental failure of leadership and, since its structure stifles any attempt at leadership by the Laity, that failure resides in Vatican City. The oligarchic model no longer is adequate and a selectively benevolent leadership, directed by the Pope and the Roman Curia, collectively referred to herein as the Vatican, under a mantle of implied infallibility is not working.

It must be said that this failure of leadership occurred because we all stood by and let it. We let the Vatican get away with the arrogance and duplicity and poor judgment that brought the current state of affairs upon us all. We didn't even try to stop it. Some left. The others coped.

From the perspective of the hierarchy, the Institutional Church has become an organization with only one major issue: Abortion. That is certainly important and I agree strongly with the premise, even stronger than *they* have stated. But the Vatican acts as if everything else is irrelevant and it is in total denial about the paralyzing effect of this attitude.

Recently, there appears to be a new denial strategy evolving. I call it Perverse Trivialization. It is the practice of exaggerating the importance of trivial things, perhaps in a bizarre effort to distract us from the more serious. Allow me to describe a recent case in point.

An article that was treated as "breaking news" appeared a few weeks ago in our local Diocesan newspaper. It is, of course very difficult in modern times for a weekly newspaper to *have* breaking news, but when the emergence of *anything* new develops as slowly as it does in the Catholic Church, perhaps it might be considered "breaking news".

Just savor this breathless lead from the article provided by the Catholic News Service, which provides most of the content in nearly every Diocesan newspaper:

> "You didn't hear these words at the end of last Sunday's Mass: 'Go in peace, glorifying the Lord by your life.' But you may well hear them the first Sunday of Advent 2011, when

the new English translation of the Roman Missal is implemented at English-speaking Masses in the United States.

Msgr. Anthony Sherman, director of the US bishop's Secretariat of Divine Worship, pointed out in an interview that these words represent one of four options in the missal for what is termed 'the dismissal' at the conclusion of the Mass. The other options are, 'Go and announce the Gospel of the Lord', 'Go in Peace' and 'Go forth, the Mass is ended'..."

Well how about that for progress!
The article goes on to say:

"Liturgical scholars and theologians long have discussed the Eucharist's dismissal, which in Latin has been worded *Ite, missa est"* ('Go, the Mass is ended'). They've made the point that these words do not mean, in effect: 'OK, leave now; we're finished'."

But apparently adding "forth" clears that up. Why of course, how imperceptive of us!

In an accompanying article also provided by CNS in this two page spread on this earth shaking development, we have the following:

"Latin is the official language of the Roman Catholic Church, recognizing its historical heritage and the fact that the church is universal.

Because Latin is no longer a living language..., the meaning of the words isn't constantly changing."

That statement accurately reflects what I remember being taught about the use of Latin, with one exception. Latin was used to preserve the *originally intended* meaning of the words.

Now, there are four approved options for the meaning of *"Ite, missa est"*. They are clearly different from one another. It must be that they also changed that fundamental belief that "Things equal to the same thing are equal to each other".

This second article from CNS also included a warning:

"Between now and when the new translation begins to be used, parishioners must be prepared for an onslaught of practice to help them get used to some of the changes.

For example, when we pray the Nicene Creed at Mass, we will have to remember to say, 'I believe' instead of 'We believe'. 'I believe' is the more accurate translation of the word *credo* that's used in the missal."

Just what is it that they think we don't get? Come on. Put the new missals in the pews when they are available. Those who use one will be able to handle the changes. Trust us. On that, we may cope, but when it comes to important stuff, watch out.

The Church, meaning we, not the Institutional Church is heading for a Howard Beale moment: "We are mad as hell and we're not going to take this anymore!"

There was a third and interesting article from CNS included in that two page spread. It dealt with the cost of the change to the new missal. Comments in parentheses are mine:

"The introduction of a new translation of the Roman Missal in parishes throughout the United States is no small undertaking. Parish leadership teams must be identified and meet to discuss how (*but not whether*) to implement the new missal.

Resources to facilitate implementation must be purchased. Priests must participate in special workshops to fully understand their role in the new guidelines. Sessions must be held to address parishioners' concerns (*although changes or exceptions will not be considered*).

What each new Roman Missal will cost will be determined by its size, number of pages, binding, art work, etc. A missal that runs 1,000 pages, for example, could cost around $100.

Then there is the matter of buying new missalettes for parishes. The missalette, which is produced monthly or seasonally and contains hymns not found in the Roman Missal, is an abbreviated version of the missal.

Is it worth all this work and expense?" (*Can this be a serious question?*)

My answer to that question is quite different from the one in the article: I suspect that the whole exercise is a money-making scam by the Institutional Church. Like NFL teams changing the design of their jerseys to sell more jerseys to the people who already have one.

There was a fourth article from CNS, which completes the two-page spread. Its content should surprise no one. A 'bargain priced' 88-page "Parish Guide to Implementing the Roman Missal, Third Edition is available for just $9.95. There is a 'can't live without' five part DVD "Become One Body, One Spirit in Christ" for a mere $19.95. Both items and many more in every price range, plus the inevitable shipping and handling are available from www.usccbpublishing.com. In the interest of full disclosure, the usccb in usccbpublishing stands for United States Council of Catholic Bishops.

If I can obtain a license from USCCB, I am considering introducing a line of "I love my New Missal" tee shirts, gym shorts, hoodies and hats for the back-to-school market before the new missal goes into use.

Please understand that I have no particular problem with changing the words of the Mass, other than the triviality of it when there are so many more important things that need changing. I am more put off by the pedantic and patronizing manner in which the change is presented. As if we were children. No, that is not correct. As if we were ignorant. That appears to be the underlying strategy: Treat them as ignorant until they begin to believe that they are ignorant.

All of this attention to the new Missal made me curious about the current one. I for one stopped reading a missal when English became the language of the Mass, preferring to pay close and undivided attention to the mystery unfolding before me rather than reading a written account of it. I thought that was the purpose of using the native language. Somehow that seems far more logical to me.

I sometimes share my attendance at Mass between two churches, which happen to be located in two different Dioceses. As the congregations enter for Mass at each of these churches there are three or four Missals at each end of each pew. I have tried to observe missal use as well as I can without being distractive.

My admittedly unscientific survey tells me that fewer than half of the congregation use missals and those who do, usually are trying to find an obscure and un-sing-able hymn, which it does not contain. However, despite this the responses of the congregations and the prayers to be recited in unison from time to time are performed quite well. One might persuasively argue that the Missals are not needed.

The new missal, like the current one is a response to the Liturgy changes made by Vatican II, some forty-five years ago. Ten years ago a dispute arose about the accuracy of the translation used thirty-five years earlier. It has apparently taken another ten years to resolve that dispute and while they were at it they added to the "richness of the liturgy". I suppose that means having five options of saying "Go, the Mass is ended". How's that for "richness"?

Only one response by the congregation is changed in the new Missal. To avoid trauma, we are going to have nearly fourteen months to learn it.

In 1936 I was six years old and had a new friend. He was a year older than I and went to parochial school. I was a public. Those of you who read my first book will remember that this was the boy whose immortal soul I saved from eternal damnation by tackling him during Mass when he tried to go to Communion because I knew that he had just eaten breakfast.

At that time, my friend was really into religion, especially the Mass. On days when the weather was inhospitable he would often insist that we "play Mass". I found that to be boring.

You see when we played Mass, since he had already made his First Holy Communion my friend was the priest. He stood facing his dresser and I was directed to kneel behind him and a little to the right, also facing the dresser. For some reason, my friend my friend wanted to be called Ed rather than his real name. But I didn't have much to do and was really not very involved.

This "priest" would jabber away in pretend Latin for several minutes at a time, but when he thought I was losing interest, he would turn around, stretch out his hands and solemnly say, "Dominus vobiscum". Neither of us knew what that meant, but I would promptly deliver my only line in this drama, "Ed, come speary tutu-oh", whatever that meant.

When the language of the Mass changed to English I learned that *Et cum spiritu tuo* meant "And with your spirit". However, the current Missal says "And also with you". So, the only new response, which we have fourteen months to learn is, drum roll, please "And with your spirit".

Don't these guys remember what Nero was doing when their hometown was burning down?

Chapter Eight

The Restoration

There have been some times while writing this book when I thought I would never finish it. Not because I lacked the energy or will to complete it, but because new, interesting and relevant material for which I wasn't even looking, kept finding me.

When I first outlined this book, it had nine chapters. Now it has fourteen. Who knows how many will be required to complete it. This chapter is one that was prompted, or rather was delivered to me at different times in two separate e-mails from friends who knew I was writing a book about today's Catholic Church, but were unaware of the details of my approach. Each of the pieces was the transcript of a speech by a different speaker, in different parts of the world. Together, they form a story that is integral to this book.

The first is a talk given on June 1, 2010 by Bishop Kevin Dowling of Rustenburg, South Africa addressing a group in Cape Town. The Bishop thought that he was speaking "off the record" but the story was leaked. *The National Catholic Reporter* picked it up and with Dowling's permission printed it.

This talk, by someone on "the inside" is such a ringing indictment of current conditions and is stated so eloquently that I request your indulgence as I quote from it liberally (no pun intended) here, rather than paraphrasing.

Ironically, Bishop Dowling began his talk with a reference to a Latin Mass celebrated by Bishop Edward Slattery of Tulsa and an article by NCR's own Jerry Filtreau. Filtreau had reported that Bishop Slattery wore a "cappa magna", which he described as a "20-yard long brilliant red train...that has come to be one of the symbols of the revival of the Tridentine Mass".

Bishop Dowling commented as follows:

"For me, such a display of what amounts to triumphalism in a church torn apart by the sexual abuse scandal, is most unfortunate. What happened there bore the marks of a medieval royal court, not the humble, servant leadership modeled by Jesus. But it seems to me that this is also a symbol of what has been happening in the church especially since pope John Paul II became the Bishop of Rome and up till today — and that is "restorationism," the carefully planned dismantling of the theology, ecclesiology, pastoral vision, indeed the "opening of the windows" of Vatican II — in order to "restore" a previous, or more controllable model of church through an increasingly centralized power structure; a structure which now controls everything in the life of the church through a network of Vatican congregations led by cardinals who ensure strict compliance with what is deemed *by them* to be "orthodox." Those who do not comply face censure and punishment, e.g. theologians who are forbidden to teach in Catholic faculties."

He then elaborated on the reason for his disdain:

"Lest we do not highlight sufficiently this important fact, Vatican II was an ecumenical council, i.e., a solemn exercise of the *magisterium* of the church, i.e. the college of bishops gathered together with the bishop of Rome and exercising a teaching function for the whole church. In other words, its vision, its principles and the direction it gave are to be followed and implemented by all, from the pope to the peasant farmer in the fields of Honduras."

I will discuss some aspects of the Magisterium in the next chapter and Bishop Dowling eloquently sets the stage for that. He talks about the selective use of Magisterium to control the faithful and maintain the dismal status quo.

"Since Vatican II there has been no such similar exercise of teaching authority by the *magisterium*. Instead, a series of decrees, pronouncements and decisions which have been given various "labels" stating, for example, that they must be firmly held to with "internal assent" by the Catholic faithful, but in reality are simply the theological or pastoral interpretations or opinions of those who have power at the centre of the church. They have not been solemnly defined as belonging to the "deposit of the faith" to be believed and followed, therefore, by all Catholics, as with other solemnly proclaimed dogmas. For example, the issues of celibacy for the priesthood and the ordination of women, are withdrawn even from the realm of discussion. Therefore, such pronouncements are open to scrutiny — to discern whether they are in accord, for example, with the fundamental theological vision of Vatican II, or whether there is indeed a case to be made for a different interpretation or opinion.

When I worked internationally from my religious congregation's base in Rome from 1985 to 1990 [Dowling is a Redemptorist] before I came back here as bishop of Rustenburg, one of my responsibilities was the building up of young adult ministry with our communities in the countries of Europe where so many of the young people were alienated from the church. I developed relationships with many hundreds of sincere, searching Catholic young adults, very open to issues of injustice, poverty and misery in the world, aware of structural injustice in the political and economic systems which dominated the world, but who increasingly felt that the "official" church was not only out of touch with reality, but a counter-witness to the aspirations of thinking and aware Catholics who sought a different experience of church. In other words, an experience which enabled them to believe that the church they belonged to had something relevant to say and to witness to in the very challenging world in which they lived. Many, many of these young adults have since left the church entirely"

He places the responsibility for the departure of "many, many of these young adults" clearly on the Restoration Movement, developed by then-Cardinal Joseph Ratzinger, sold to Pope John Paul II and sponsored by the Curia:

"On the other hand, it has to be recognized that for a significant number of young Catholics, adult Catholics, priests and religious around the world, the "restorationist" model of church which has been implemented over the past 30-40 years is sought after and valued; it meets a need in them; it gives them a feeling of belonging to something with very clear parameters and guidelines for living, thus giving them a sense of security and clarity about what is truth and what is morally right or wrong, because there is a clear and strong authority structure which decides definitively on all such questions, and which they trust absolutely as being of divine origin.

The rise of conservative groups and organizations in the church over the past 40 years and more, which attract significant numbers of adherents, has led to a phenomenon which I find difficult to deal with, viz. an inward looking church, fearful of if not antagonistic towards a secularist world with its concomitant danger of relativism especially in terms of truth and morality — frequently referred to by pope Benedict XVI; a church which gives an impression of "retreating behind the wagons," and relying on a strong central authority to ensure unity through uniformity in belief and praxis in the face of such dangers. The fear is that without such supervision and control, and that if any freedom in decision-making is allowed, even in less important matters, this will open the door to division and a breakdown in the unity of the church.

This is all about a fundamentally different "vision" *in* the church and "vision" *of* the church. Where today can we find the great theological leaders and thinkers of the past, like Cardinal [Joseph] Frings of Cologne, Germany...who in today's world "out there" even listens to, much less appreciates and allows themselves to be challenged by the leadership of the church at the present time?"

It is interesting and perhaps not unintentional that Dowling mentions Cardinal Frings, who was *clearly a proponent for change* at Vatican II. The Peritus, or theological consultant assigned to the Cardinal during the Council was the same Rev. Josef Alois Ratzinger, now Pope Benedict XVI. Dowling continues:

> "I think the moral authority of the church's leadership today has never been weaker. It is, therefore, important in my view that church leadership, instead of giving an impression of its power, privilege and prestige, should rather be experienced as a humble, searching ministry together with its people in order to discern the most appropriate or viable responses which can be made to complex ethical and moral questions — a leadership, therefore, which does not presume to have all the answers all the time."

The Bishop acknowledges certain contributions of the Popes since Vatican II in the area of Social Teaching, but with a caveat:

> "But to change focus a bit. One of the truly significant contributions of the church to the building up of a world in which people and communities can live in peace and dignity, with a quality of life which befits those made in God's image, has been the body of what has been called "Catholic Social Teaching", a compendium of which has been released during the past few years. These social teaching principles are: The Common Good, Solidarity, The Option for the Poor, Subsidiarity, The Common Destiny of Goods, The Integrity of Creation, and People-Centeredness — all based on and flowing out of the values of the Gospel..."

> "...However, if church leadership anywhere presumes to criticize or critique socio-political-economic policies and policy makers, or governments, it must also allow itself to be critiqued in the same way in terms of its policies, its internal life, and especially its modus operandi. A democratic culture and praxis, with its focus on the participation of citizens and holding accountable those who are elected to govern, is increasingly appreciated in spite of inevitable human short-

comings. When thinking people of all persuasions look at church leadership, they raise questions about, for example, real participation of the membership in its governance and how in fact church leadership is to be held accountable, and to whom...Let us take one social teaching principle, vitally important for ensuring participative democracy in the socio-political domain, viz. subsidiarity..."

"...The principle of subsidiarity protects the rights of individuals and groups in the face of the powerful, especially the state. It holds that those things which can be done or decided at a lower level of society should not be taken over by a higher level. As such, it reaffirms our right and our capacity to decide for ourselves how to organise our relationships and how to enter into agreements with others. ... We can and should take steps to encourage decision-making at lower levels of the economy, and to empower the greatest number of people to participate as fully as possible in economic life."

Then he addresses the principle of subsidiarity applied to post-Vatican II ecclesiology:

"...Applied to the church, the principle of subsidiarity requires of its leadership to actively promote and encourage participation, personal responsibility and effective engagement by everyone in terms of their particular calling and ministry in the church and world according to their opportunities and gifts.

However, I think that today we have a leadership in the church which actually undermines the very notion of subsidiarity; where the minutiae of church life and praxis "at the lower level" are subject to examination and authentication being given by the "higher level," in fact the highest level, e.g., the approval of liturgical language and texts; where one of the key Vatican II principles, collegiality in decision-making, is virtually non-existent. The eminent emeritus Archbishop of Vienna, Cardinal Franz König, wrote the following in 1999 — almost 35 years after Vatican II: "In fact, however, *de facto* and not *de jure*, intentionally or unintentionally, the curial authorities working in conjunction with the pope have appropriated the tasks of the episcopal college. It is they who now carry out almost all of them" ("My Vision of the church of the Future", *The Tablet*, March 27, 1999, p. 434).

"What compounds this, for me, is the mystique which has in increasing measure surrounded the person of the pope in the last 30 years, such that any hint of critique or questioning of his policies, his way of thinking, his exercise of authority etc. is equated with disloyalty. There is more than a perception, because of this mystique, that unquestioning obedience by the faithful to the pope is required and is a sign of the ethos and fidelity of a true Catholic. When the pope's authority is then intentionally extended to the Vatican curia, there exists a real possibility that unquestioning obedience to very human decisions about a whole range of issues by the curial departments and cardinals also becomes a mark of one's fidelity as a Catholic, and anything less is interpreted as being disloyal to the pope who is charged with steering the bark of Peter.

It has become more and more difficult over the past years, therefore, for the College of Bishops as a whole, or in a particular territory, to exercise their theologically-based servant leadership to discern appropriate responses to their particular socio-economic, cultural, liturgical, spiritual and other pastoral realities and needs; much less to disagree with or seek alternatives to policies and decisions taken in Rome. And what appears to be more and more the policy of appointing "safe", unquestionably orthodox and even very conservative bishops to fill vacant dioceses over the past 30 years, only makes it less and less likely that the College of Bishops — even in powerful conferences like the United States — will question what comes out of Rome, and certainly not publicly. Instead, there will be every effort to try and find an accommodation with those in power, which means that the Roman position will prevail in the end. And, taking this further, when an individual bishop takes issue with something, especially in public, the impression or judgment will be that he is "breaking ranks" with the other bishops and will only cause confusion to the lay faithful — so it is said - because it will appear that the bishops are not united in their teaching and leadership role. The pressure, therefore, is to conform.

What we should have, in my view, is a church where the leadership recognizes and empowers decision-making at the appropriate levels in the local church; where local leadership listens to and discerns with the people of God of that area what "the Spirit is saying to the church" and then articulates that as a consensus of the believing, praying, serving community. It needs faith in God and trust in the people of God to take what may seem to some or many as a risk. The church could be enriched as a result through a diversity which truly integrates socio-cultural values and insights into a living and developing faith, together with a discernment of how such diversity can promote unity in the church — and not, therefore, require uniformity to be truly authentic.

Diversity in living and praxis, as an expression of the principle of subsidiarity, has been taken away from the local churches everywhere by the centralization of decision-making at the level of the Vatican. In addition, orthodoxy is more and more identified with conservative opinions and outlook, with the corresponding judgment that what is perceived to be "liberal" is both suspect and not orthodox, and therefore to be rejected as a danger to the faith of the people.

Is there a way forward? I have grappled with this question especially in the light of the apparent division of aspiration and vision in the church. How do you reconcile such very different visions of church, or models of church? I do not have the answer, except that somewhere we must find an attitude of respect and reverence for difference and diversity as we search for a *living* unity in the church; that people be allowed, indeed enabled, to find or create the type of community which is expressive of their faith and aspirations concerning their Christian and Catholic lives and engagement in church and world, and which strives to hold in legitimate and constructive tension the uncertainties and ambiguities that all this will bring, trusting in the presence of the Holy Spirit.

At the heart of this is the question of conscience. As Catholics, we need to be trusted enough to make informed decisions about our life, our witness, our expressions of faith, spirituality, prayer, and involvement in the world —

on the basis of a developed conscience. And, as an invitation to an appreciation of conscience and conscientious decisions about life and participation in what is a very human church, I close with the formulation or understanding given by none other than the theologian, Fr. Josef Ratzinger, now pope, when he was a *peritus*, or expert, at Vatican II:

> "Over the pope as expression of the binding claim of ecclesiastical authority, there stands one's own conscience which must be obeyed before all else, even if necessary against the requirement of ecclesiastical authority. This emphasis on the individual, whose conscience confronts him with a supreme and ultimate tribunal, and one which in the last resort is beyond the claim of external social groups, even the official church, also establishes a principle in opposition to increasing totalitarianism".
>
> (Josef Ratzinger in: Commentary on the Documents of Vatican II, Vol. V., pg. 134 (Ed) H. Vorgrimler, New York, Herder and Herder, 1967)."

The question is now begged: How did this Restoration movement happen? That brings us to the second speech and the other speaker. The speech, which will be covered in Chapter Twelve is not relevant here. However the speaker, Robert Blair Kaiser is, because of a book he wrote.

Robert Blair Kaiser was in Rome throughout Vatican II, as a correspondent covering the Council for Time Magazine. He returned to Rome during the last days of Pope John Paul II and stayed through the conclave that elected his successor, Joseph Ratzinger as Benedict XVI.

During this second period, he studied several Cardinals including Cardinal Ratzinger and the papal election process. Those studies produced a fascinating book *A Church in Search of Itself: Benedict XVI and the Battle for the Future.*

Obviously, the book is about the rise of Josef Cardinal Ratzinger to the highest office in the Catholic Church, but the remarkable thing is how long ago it was planned. Therein is the secret of how we finally arrived at where we are.

In his earlier years, then Father Ratzinger was an academic of some prominence and during Vatican II he served as Peritus to the Archbishop of Cologne, Germany Joseph Frings. From the perspective of today, that assignment seems quite ironic.

In his book *What Happened at Vatican II*, John W. O'Malley, SJ describes Ratzinger as "among the more important young Theologians at the Council, carrying considerable weight with the German Bishops".

O'Malley describes Frings as "a powerful spokesman for the majority". In O'Malley's terms the "majority" always refers to those who favored significant change in the Church. My compliant Catholic friends translate "majority" as "liberal".

One of the most telling episodes described by O'Malley regarding Frings' position on matters occurred during a debate on collegiality. It is considered one of the most dramatic events of the four-year Second Vatican Council.

Simply stated, the majority of the Bishops felt that the governance on the Church should be conducted by the Pope *in council with* all of the Bishops rather than merely in conjunction with the Supreme Congregation of the Holy Office. The Cardinals and Bishops of the Curia obviously disagreed.

O'Malley describes that key speech by Frings during that debate:

"(Frings) speech, written in part by Ratzinger, created a sensation..."

"Then, he delivered his bombshell, an attack on the whole centralizing tendency in the church but specifically on the

Holy Office. Frings noted that an appendix to the schema provided a list of powers that the Holy See might concede to the Bishops. That, he said, got things backward. What was needed, rather, was a list of the powers reserved to the Holy See. Frings' proposition was a turnaround of the basic assumption on which the schema was based: the Holy See is the source of all power in the church.

In another appendix, moreover, the schema provided rules according which the Congregations should henceforth operate. These rules, Frings insisted, should be moved from the appendix to the main text and be understood to apply to all the Congregations (of the Curia) "even to the Supreme Congregation of the Holy Office, whose procedures many times are inappropriate to the times in which we live, harm the church and are for many a scandal". Applause broke out – *plausus in aula*, as the official record states. Not even by that Congregation, he went on, should anyone be condemned without being heard.

(Cardinal) Ottaviani (Secretary of the Holy Office), already scheduled to speak that day, prefaced his remarks with an extemporaneous reply to Frings. He protested to the highest degree the words against the Supreme Congregation of the Holy Office, whose president, he reminded the fathers, was the pope himself. The words sprang from ignorance – lest he give offense by using a stronger expression – yes from ignorance about how careful the Holy Office was to inquire broadly among experts before the members came to a conclusion and sent it to the Pontiff for ratification."

Eventually, nearly two years later Paul VI established the Synod of Bishops, a watered down version of Collegiality, which effectively took the issue off the Vatican II table. The Synod of Bishops has proven as ineffectual as it had been planned to be. This was a major setback in the battle for change in the Church.

It should be noted that at the same time, Pope VI renamed Supreme Congregation of the Holy Office as the Congregation for the Doctrine of the Faith. Sixteen years later, the peritus of Archbishop Frings was named Prefect the Congregation for the Doctrine of the Faith by

Pope John Paul II. Will the real Josef Ratzinger please stand up, or did he?

In his book *A Church in Search of Itself*, Robert Blair Kaiser says that Ratzinger's epiphany came in 1968 when he became concerned that Communism would replace Christianity in Europe. That confirmed his misgivings about the Vatican II document Gaudium et Spes, which urged Christians to become more involved in the world.

Over time he became more and more dedicated to returning the Church to its pre-Vatican II positions, particularly in the reducing efforts toward ecumenism and minimizing collegiality. Paul VI, who had never really accepted the vision and promise of John XXIII in convening the Second Vatican Council and had tried to control its outcome saw the brilliant young German as an ally in an effort to undo some, if not all of the advances made by Vatican II. The movement that Bishop Dowling described in his speech quoted earlier as "The Restoration" had begun.

In 1977 Paul VI made the fifty year-old Father Ratzinger Archbishop of Munich and a Cardinal. Later, in 1981 Pope John Paul II appointed him Prefect of the Congregation of the Doctrine of the Faith, the very post which he had helped Cardinal Frings attack.

Cardinal Ratzinger's power and his influence over John Paul II grew steadily over the ensuing years and in 2002 he was confirmed as Dean of the College of Cardinals, the person who would manage the *inter-regnum* when the Pope died and heavily influence the selection of his successor.

We will probably never know just how much of the reign of John Paul II was his and how much was Cardinal Ratzinger speaking and acting through him. Most people would agree that the John Paul who entered the Papacy was quite different from the one who left it. Did he really change or was that change subtly engineered by the driven Ratzinger to further his own ambitions?

Kaiser described the analysis of that phenomenon by author and long time Vatican reporter for the Rome daily *La Repubblica*, Marco Politi this way:

> "He saw a connection between a whole series of backward steps in the Vatican through the summer of the Jubilee year 2000, ending with *Dominus Jesus* (Cardinal Ratzinger's book) that proved that Ratzinger and a few like-minded prelates in the Curia were doing everything possible to tie the hands of any possibly more liberal successor to the papacy."

The result of that effort had a short term result as well, right up to the Pope's death in April 2005. Kaiser again:

> "By 2005, Rome had never had so much power, not during the record-breaking thirty-two year reign of Pius IX in the nineteenth century, not during the reign of the three Piuses of the early twentieth century.
>
> Much of the power was funneled into the suppression of free speech in the Church and free inquiry by theologians who had felt empowered by the open charter written by the Fathers of Vatican II. Rome could encouraged right-wing lay movements like *Focolare, Communion and Liberation,* and *The Neocatechumenal Way* [all three of them under the covert control of clerics] and give a great deal of grief to the most rambunctious religious orders [which didn't have to answer to local bishops, but only bucked them at their own political peril] and to organizations like *Call to Action* and *Voice of the Faithful.*
>
> Local bishops found it easy to marginalize these largely lay groups by decreeing that they could not meet in Church-owned parish halls – or worse: in 1996, Bishop Fabian Bruskewitz, overly sure of himself, excommunicated members of *Call to Action* in his Diocese of Lincoln, Nebraska...

And no bishop ever dared criticize. The Church – the hierarchical Church, at least – was in Ratzinger's pocket. If he had his way, the conclave (to elect a new Pope) would not turn its back on the perfection that he and John Paul had achieved."

Kaiser's book chronicles what he considers to be Cardinal Ratzinger's campaign to *become* that successor, which began long before John Paul II's death. Kaiser suggests that Ratzinger's strategy was to identify himself so completely with John Paul II (or at least to the image of John Paul, which Cardinal Ratzinger created) that it appears to the electors that the only way to carry on the work of John Paul II is to elect the Cardinal as his successor.

Of course, in the mind of Cardinal Ratzinger the work of John Paul II was to dismantle the vision of John XXIII and take the Church back to the nineteenth century.

It is an extraordinary story.

Kaiser says that the politicking began in earnest during the grieving period for John Paul:

"Had this great crowd come for their love of this Pope?... that's what members of *Communion and Liberation* wanted everyone to think. Not twenty-four hours after the death of the Pope they were out in the streets with a brochure claiming the last loving words of the Pope before he died: 'I looked for you. Now you have come to me. And I thank you'. According to Renato Buzzonetti, the pope's physician, John Paul II was unable to speak for some days before he expired. So these words were a concoction, designed to play up John Paul's greatness even on his deathbed. Make him a ghostly presence at the conclave and you help to assure the continuation of his programs and policies.

The leaders of Focolare decided they could do that best by promoting a campaign for the immediate proclamation of John Paul's sainthood. They planted a banner on the set of Porta a Porta, Rome's most popular television talk show that read SANTO SUBITO, 'Saint Now'. In the next few days, the same SANTO SUBITO banners popped up all over town."

We all know how effective that has been. The new Pope has put John Paul on the fast track to sainthood in an apparent attempt to pre-empt the contributions of the visionary John XXIII by having John Paul II reach sainthood first.

It must be remembered that while Vatican II was attended by more than 3,000 bishops and cardinals, each with a vote to cast, the Pope is elected only by those Cardinals who are under the age of eighty. There were only 115 eligible to vote in 2005 and since John Paul had been Pope for twenty-eight years, he had appointed most of them and they owed their entire careers to him. There were certainly more than the seventy-seven needed to elect Cardinal Ratzinger.

Think of that. Seventy-seven men determine the leadership for life of more than a billion people.

Kaiser relates this about the managing of the Pope's funeral by the Cardinal:

> "As dean of the College of Cardinals, he (Ratzinger) was the principal celebrant at the mass. He could have delegated anyone to give the homily. That he didn't should have been a clue that Ratzinger was intent on making his leadership known to two audiences: (1) the largest chunk of humanity that had ever watched a funeral together and (2) a tiny group of 115 cardinal electors goggling at an unusual show of rhetoric and power on the part of the man they had always known as entirely soft-spoken and shy.

> But this was a crucial time in the passing of papal power and no time for Ratzinger to be timid. He made the most of his opportunity, not to deliver a theological reflection on heaven and hell to this very mixed audience, but to tell stories about Karol Wojtyla and his spiritual journey. He ended his narrative with a confession of his feelings for John Paul II. 'Today we bury his remains in the earth as a seed of immortality. Our hearts are full of sadness, yet at the same time of joyful hope and profound gratitude'."

Kaiser titled his chapter on the Conclave, "One Smart Move After Another" and indeed it was, from "forgetting" to provide translators during the preliminary getting acquainted sessions so that language challenged Cardinals had difficulty in learning about each other; to recognizing that "to get the job you had to want the job"; to making friends and flattering groups like the Africans, who knew that none of their members would be considered; to making it clear to all that "Increasingly over the past four years, he had become a virtual incumbent, making most of the papal decisions, writing many of the papal speeches, acting behind the scenes in ways the pope could not".

He tried to cut the cardinal electors off from talking with the press in an effort to limit the effect of outside, albeit informed opinions on those who would be casting the crucial ballots.

During this pre-conclave period the Cardinal did a curious and somewhat bold thing. Kaiser describes it:

"On April 14, Ratzinger decided to gauge his electoral strength and consented to let his closest supporters in the college...circulate a sign-up sheet in the Paul VI Synod Hall, where the cardinals held their morning meetings. If the sheet did not come back with fifty names on it, Ratzinger would take himself out of the running. According to an aide to one of the Brazilian cardinals, it came back 'with almost forty names'. For Ratzinger, that was enough to make a substantial showing on the first ballot. Forty votes was not enough to win. He needed seventy-seven. But it was an encouraging start.

Other cardinals were alarmed. The three top Italian reporters at the Vatican...came up with separate reports from inside the conclave that eight of the Americans and four of the Germans had seen the sheet going around, stunned now to see the first real evidence that Ratzinger's seizing center stage at every turn was not only an exercise of leadership but a grab for power, too. He wanted the papacy."

Then, on the first day of the Conclave, when the 115 cardinal electors were to be sequestered to deliberate and note Cardinal Ratzinger again used the platform provided by the Mass. Once again, instead of delegating the delivery of the homily, he reserved that task to himself.

Kaiser describes it as "his campaign speech" and tells his readers:

> "Ratzinger prayed God would give the Church 'a new pope, like John Paul II, who will guide us to the love of Christ'. The new pope would do that by making sure the faithful would not be 'tossed about and carried here and there by any doctrinal wind'. He didn't explain what a 'doctrinal wind' was, but quickly shifted his metaphor. The real danger was more like a series of waves that tossed people about 'from one end to the other'.

> Then he ticked off a litany of scary abstractions that had long marked Ratzinger's rhetoric: Marxism, liberalism, libertinism, collectivism, radical individualism, atheism, religious mysticism, agnosticism, syncretism – while anyone who opposed these popular modern 'isms' were charged with another 'ism', fundamentalism, a word of contempt in most quarters, but one Ratzinger used triumphantly and unequivocally. For him, fundamentalism was 'a clear faith, according to the creed of the Church'. By that definition, he was a fundamentalist and proud of it."

Thus the Conclave began. On the first ballot Ratzinger received forty-seven votes; Bergoglio, ten; Montini, nine; Ruini, six; Sodano, four; Rodriguez Maradiaga, three; and Tettamanzi, two. That evening Montini withdrew for health reasons.

On the second ballot Ratzinger had sixty-five votes, more than a simple majority; Bergoglio, who would have been the first Latin American and first Jesuit, had thirty-five. On the third, Ratzinger edged closer with seventy-two, just five short and Bergoglio reached forty.

Later that day, on the fourth ballot it was over. Ratzinger received eighty-four votes and became Pope Benedict XVI. Although the victory was impressive, it was not popular with all the electors. Ten cardinals boy-cotted the celebratory dinner. One of them was quoted in answer to a question, "No, we don't have to accept the Pope's theology. It may change. I hope it does. I change my theology every day, according to the things I see happening around me. Otherwise, I wouldn't be a very good theologian".

That having been said, the Restoration remained intact and there were several early signs of its continued strength related in Kaiser's book *A Church in Search of Itself.* Two of these had been initiated even before the death of John Paul II

The first was essentially an affirmation of his pre-conclave secret pledge to not undertake any reform of the Curia, which was manifested in one of his first official acts. He announced William J. Levada, former Archbishop of San Francisco as his own replacement as Prefect of the Holy Office. Kaiser quotes a leader of SNAP (Survivors Network of Those Abused by Priests) as saying:

"(Levada) very much falls in line with how the Catholic Church has handled the problem. They've denied it. When they say he's an expert, he's only an expert on their way of dealing with things. In that way, he'll fit right in."

Kaiser also relates that "when Jim Jenkins...(the) psychologist who chaired Levada's lay review board in San Francisco, learned how Levada was handling sex-abuse protocols, he resigned" and wrote that Benedict had also quickly settled an old score with a long time critic (italics are mine):

"On May 6, Thomas J. Reese told some five hundred media people in an e-mail that he was resigning after seven years as editor of America magazine. Many believed that this was a routine move; the normal term of office for a Jesuit supe-rior is six years...Reese had been sacked by none other than Cardinal Ratzinger, just two weeks before he became Benedict XVI...those who had been willing to give...(him) a chance to show how he could be kinder as a pope than he was as an inquisitor general...wondered what Reese had done to deserve this..."

"In 2002...Reese wrote an editorial that called for the end of the Holy Office as presently run; in that piece, he wasn't attacking "Church teaching", but he was attacking Ratzinger himself...Ratzinger told (the Jesuit Superior General) that Reese would have to resign or submit every issue of the magazine to a board of censors appointed by the American bishops..."

"Tom Reese felt the magazine had a duty to express reasoned opinions on a whole range of ethical issues – and on a good many Church issues that were open questions. Cardinal Ratzinger didn't agree. For him, once the magisterium took a position on anything having to do with faith, morals *or church discipline*, it was no longer an open question..."

"So (after the Conclave) Reese resigned. Benedict XVI had the kind of electoral mandate to do anything he wanted with the Jesuits...he could take Vatican Radio out of their hands and give it to Opus Dei, which would be happy to take control of the world's largest single radio operation...or he could give Opus Dei direction over the Jesuits' Gregorian University and the Biblical Institute, still the most prestigious training ground in Rome for future bishops..."

And Benedict XVI is not finished. Sadly.

Chapter Nine

Issues of Governance

So far, several times we have mentioned the Governance of the Institutional Church, which we will discuss more thoroughly in this chapter; and the Discipline of the Institutional Church, which will be covered in the same way in the next two. Each of these terms refers to man-made regulations rather than matters of Faith and Morals based on divine revelation and/or tradition although in some cases an attempt at a connection has been made. Before we go further, let us further clarify the term Governance.

Governance (as used in this book) deals with the organizational and administrative policies and practices of the Institutional Church, which have been imposed on it by the hierarchy, from the Pope down through the parish priest. It is the way the Institutional Church conducts its business.

From the beginning of this book I have said that I do not have any serious issues with the Roman Catholic Church regarding basic Faith and Morals, but when it comes to Governance and particularly with regard to Discipline I have quite a few. I believe that is also the case with most practicing Catholics although they often do not make that distinction, often because they don't understand it. I have much more to say on this subject and will do so in the next chapter.

Most Catholics would agree that the Governance issue which affects them personally to the greatest degree is the increasingly severe failure of the Institutional Church to deliver the services they need, want, have been accustomed to receiving and deserve. This is due of course to the shortage of priests resulting from a dramatic decline in vocations over the past sixty years.

The Eucharist is becoming less available; the remaining parish priests are overworked; and expensive facilities are being abandoned, sometimes at significant expense. Despite this reality, the Institutional Church barely gives lip service to the problem and when they do it is to reject obvious solutions out of hand.

This is not just about the emotional trauma of families witnessing the closing a beloved neighborhood church and school, where they have been educated and celebrated baptisms, first communions, confirmations, marriages and funerals. It is not just about the inconvenience of having to travel an additional fifteen minutes or half an hour to attend Mass. It is about the death knell of a culture and tradition that connects the faithful to the Faith.

Recruiting efforts for Seminarians in most dioceses are pathetically ineffective. However, three perfectly viable solutions are available which receive little or no interest or attention. They are dramatic, but not cataclysmic, changes in the priesthood. The purpose and the mission remain the same, only the providers are different.

The solutions are of course, three sub-issues: elimination of celibacy as a requirement for Diocesan priests; allowing women to receive Holy Orders; and creating a higher and select level of the Deaconate allowing them to consecrate the Eucharist and celebrate Mass. All three should be adopted immediately since it will take several years to fully implement them and a great many more to catch up. They are simple and easy to understand and now is not the time to dither over them and debate, but to take action and to do that with vigor and enthusiasm.

Celibacy

Celibacy is the most mentioned by Catholics of all perspectives as the principal cause for the shortage of priests and therefore many other problems of the Church. Removing the requirement of celibacy for priests, bishops, cardinals and even the Pope is not only deemed desirable but essential for the future existence of the Church. It also would have significant symbolic importance, indicating clearly that the Institutional Church is finally willing to adapt in order to survive.

Historically, of course a married clergy is not new. Peter's mother-in-law graces the pages of the New Testament. In fact, according to the Catholic Encyclopedia, celibacy for priests and bishops was not introduced until after the Council of Nicaea in 325 AD and it was very slow to catch on over the next several centuries. Today some of the autochthonous Eastern churches in communion with the Pope, allow married clergy. The current Pope and his predecessors have also accommodated married Anglican Church priests who convert and want to be Catholic priests.

In fact, the proximate cause for the institution of celibacy was not a belief that it would make priests and bishops holier, but to prevent their children from inheriting the property they had accumulated in their parishes and dioceses. It is absurd to consider this a faith and morals issue. It is purely and simply a matter of governance.

I sense that over time many if not most Catholics would accept, if not welcome the concept of a married clergy. However, I also sense that they are not all talking about the same thing and that there a number of related issues that no one is talking about at all. It is essential at this point that we are all agreed on what eliminating celibacy *means*, so that we do not create a terrible mess.

My observation is that while most of the lay people favoring this step say, "Priests should be allowed to marry", the few in the hierarchy who lean that way say, "Perhaps we should consider *the ordination of married men*". Those two statements are poles apart in meaning and practice.

Let me make the policy I am suggesting absolutely clear. Married men should be allowed to enter the Seminary and unmarried Seminarians should be allowed to marry after ordination. Unmarried priests should be allowed to marry and married priests whose marriages are properly annulled or whose wives have died should be allowed to marry again. No false equivocation. The same rules should be extended to deacons and nuns.

I have long suspected, but am unable to prove it, that the Institutional Church's aversion to doing away with celibacy has more to do with economics than theology. The consensus of about ten surveys that I was able to find was that the range in salaries for priests is between $10,000 and $30,000, with most priests at the lower end. For tax purposes they also must count as income their car allowances and lodging provided. A married priest could not live on that unless he had a part-time second job, his wife had a well-paying career and they were *required* to practice the most effective birth control available.

Now suppose the Institutional Church increased the salaries for married priests to the level earned by people of equal education and social stature in the community, which seems only proper. Under the principle of equal pay for equal work shouldn't the unmarried priests expect comparable compensation? Are these the real reasons why we still have a celibacy requirement?

Then there is the question of housing. Removing celibacy from the requirements would seem to render the concept of a parish rectory obsolete for a variety of reasons, although some could be retained for priests *choosing* celibacy or those unable to find mates.

Despite these few economic issues, it is my opinion that it is essential to the well being of the Church to remove the requirement of celibacy for Catholic priests. That time has come.

*****

Just a few days following the completion of my final edit of this chapter, an article on the front page of the Rochester Democrat & Chronicle for Sunday, June 12, 2011 prompted an afterthought on this issue.

A fifty year old man had been ordained a priest of the Rochester Diocese the previous day.

Besides his age, what made the event unique was that the man has been married for 28 years, his wife is still living and they have six children (8 through 27), all of whom participated in the Mass. He is a professor at Roberts Wesleyan College and has served as a minister in Congregational, Reformed, Presbyterian and Baptist churches.

The article was sketchy on the details of the process but it was said that ordination came only after *he received special permission from the Vatican.* A Senior Research Associate from the Center for Applied Research in the Apostolate at Georgetown University was quoted as saying about this, "Many of them have been former Episcopalians, but there have been exceptions made for Lutherans and Baptists as well. It ends up being only one handful every year, so it is still pretty rare to see".

One can only be happy for the new priest, but some very serious questions are begged.

If all it took to make this happen was permission from the Pope, was this man the only one worthy of such consideration?

Was he for some reason deemed significantly holier and more deserving than the thousands of young Catholic men in the country who would jump at that same opportunity? Dare we ask in what ways, so they can improve?

If all it takes is the stroke of the Papal pen why hasn't the problem of the shortage of priests been solved long ago?

Why isn't the demand for answers to these questions as great as the joy at the ordination of this worthy man?

Women Priests

This is another contentious issue, with the added baggage of the traditional treatment of women as second class members of the Church. Historically there is precedence for it and as a practical matter, according to the February 2011 issue of US Catholic if all the women who now work in key positions in the Church, paid or otherwise were to quit, the Church would have to cease operations.

There is no historical impediment toward women in the priesthood. There were women serving as deacons in the early Church and many scholars believe that they carried out all the duties of priests, including consecration of the Eucharist.

There certainly are no intellectual or educational impediments either. In fact, the addition of women to the priesthood might actually increase the average IQ of the group. Once again, it is ridiculous to consider this a faith and morals issue unless one would like to argue that women, by virtue of gender are either not holy enough or not worthy enough to be ordained, or both.

Women should be permitted to become deacons or priests. And yes, if a male priest or deacon and a female priest or deacon were to fall in love and be otherwise eligible, they should be allowed to marry and not just be directed to take a cold shower.

Once again, I believe that it is time for the Institutional Church to open the diaconate and the priesthood to qualified women.

Increased Ecclesiastic Faculties for Selected Deacons

Of the three recommended remedies to alleviate the shortage of Priests, this one would seem to be the easiest to accept by the Institutional Church, since all priests become deacons at a certain point in their training. I understand that the modern deacons who have become common in our parishes today are *permanent* deacons, with limited ecclesiastic faculties. I also understand that there are probably many deacons who find their current roles completely satisfying and are not interested in becoming priests. I am not suggesting a change in this.

I am, however suggesting that *a specially selected and volunteer group* of perhaps no more than fifteen to twenty percent of all deacons be granted the additional privileges to consecrate the Eucharist, celebrate Mass and to do whatever else is deemed appropriate.

The mechanics of implementing this change appear to be administrative and rather simple. The modern Diaconate was established simply in 1967, following Vatican II by an apostolic letter from Paul VI entitled Sacram Diaconatus Ordinem. It took just one year for the United States Conference of Bishops to begin work to restore the role of deacons in the United States, perhaps their quickest response to anything in history. It would seem that this new level of the Diaconate could be implemented administratively in very short order by merely amending that apostolic letter and that the additional training could be completed in less than a year or two.

This would have an almost immediate impact on the shortage of Priests. However, it is not the whole answer, which requires the use of the other two remedies, elimination of Celibacy and Ordination of Women, although it would certainly buy some time for their implementation.

I believe that the concept of additional faculties for selected deacons should be immediately considered and hopefully adopted.

Bishops

Bishops may be the major problem with the Church, but they *could* be the major contributors to its recovery. There is no question that administratively and organizationally we need bishops, but they need a brand new job description, attitude and purpose. The most disturbing element of this situation is that apparently the bishops don't have a clue that they are a problem.

Bishops currently represent an almost impenetrable upward communications barrier between the hierarchy and the more than a billion ordinary Catholics, and their downward communications are hardly better. They claim to be pastoral when they are really juridical. They often do not appear to be from, of, or with the people, but indifferent, superior and disdainful of them.

Examples of this are all around us, from the misguided Archbishop of Phoenix mentioned in Chapter Two who excommunicated that nun for saving a pregnant woman's life and then declared her hospital no longer Catholic; to the misinformed USCCB who came out against Health Care Reform because it paid for abortions when in truth existing Federal Law prohibits that and then ignored the two orders of nuns who had it correct; to those who withhold the Eucharist from elected officials who personally reject the concept of abortion, but carry out their sworn duty to represent the will of their constituents; to the dozens who are personally guilty of sexual abuse toward children or at least have participated in covering it up; and to all of those who believe that "avoiding the semblance of scandal" is infinitely more important than doing the right thing.

Knowing the Institutional Church as we do, certainly there is no one who seriously believes that these are rogue prelates acting on their own without at least tacit approval, if not direction from those in more exalted levels of the hierarchy. That is evident when one considers that one of the more negatively notable of those involved in the sexual abuse cover-up, was allowed to resign as Archbishop of Boston without public censure; was then rewarded with a cushy job in the Vatican; and now is one of the thirty-five members of the Congregation of Bishops, charged with the responsibility of examining candidates for their suitability to become bishops. What does he know about that?

The cynicism of the Institutional Church is extraordinary although I don't really believe that all the bishops want it to be that way. That is clearly not what Christ had in mind, when he compared Peter to a rock upon which a Church would be built.

Among the key elements of the solution, which also could be implemented by a simple pastoral letter from an enlightened Pope are: Bishops should be chosen from their home diocese; they should be elected by the members of that diocese and merely approved by the Pope; their primary task should be the *upward* communication of the wants and needs of the people under their jurisdiction; and they should fairly represent those people at whatever meetings, Synods or Ecumenical Councils they attend.

This subject is treated in much more detail in Chapter Eleven, A Large First Step.

This places the selection of a bishop where it was historically until the past few centuries and where it logically belongs. Papal appointment of bishops is not traditional. Father Richard McBrien is the Crowley-O'Brien professor of theology at the University of Notre Dame, Indiana. The following is excerpted from his column in the April 17, 2009 issue of the *National Catholic Reporter*:

"Throughout most of the history of the Catholic church, bishops were elected from the local diocesan clergy by laity and clergy alike. The bishop of Rome had no direct role whatsoever in those elections.

However, because of the communion that existed, and still exists, among all the local churches, or dioceses, both with one another and with the diocese of Rome and its bishop, the pope was subsequently informed of the results of these elections as a matter of courtesy and protocol.

It was not until the 19th century, however, that the popes began to claim the exclusive right to appoint bishops throughout the Catholic world. Although the pope has exercised this prerogative ever since then, it is hardly traditional.

Catholics in the first millennium would have been taken aback by the papal appointments of bishops, but they would have been utterly shocked to learn that someone who was already the bishop of one diocese would accept election to another.

Such a practice would have been recognized as being in direct violation of the teaching of the First Council of Nicaea in 325, the council that defined the divinity of Jesus Christ and gave us the Nicene Creed. Nicaea's teaching was reaffirmed by the Council of Chalcedon in 451, the council that defined the relationship between the divinity and humanity of Christ.

Canon 15 of Nicaea reads as follows:

'On account of the great disturbance and the factions which are caused, it is decreed that the custom, if it is found to exist in some parts contrary to the canon, shall be totally suppressed, so that neither bishops nor presbyters [priests] nor deacons shall transfer from city to city.

If after this decision of this holy and great synod anyone shall attempt such a thing, or shall lend himself to such a proceeding, the arrangement shall be totally annulled, and he shall be restored to the church of which he was ordained bishop or presbyter or deacon.'

The Council of Chalcedon, 126 years later, reiterated the teaching of Nicaea in its own Canon 6:

'In the matter of bishops or clerics who move from city to city, it has been decided that the canons issued by the holy fathers concerning them should retain proper force.'

These two canons, which have never been explicitly revoked, were consistently regarded as retaining "their proper force" as late as the year 897, when the body of Pope Formosus (891-96) was exhumed from its resting place nine months after his death. The body was clothed in full pontifical vestments and placed on trial in what became known as the "cadaver synod."

Among the charges leveled against the deceased pope was that he had accepted election as bishop of Rome when he was already the bishop of another diocese (Porto, Italy), in clear violation of the canons of the councils of Nicaea and Chalcedon.

It is significant, however, that no known protest had been registered at the time of his election to Rome...The force of these canons obviously did not endure into the second or third Christian millennium, when the practice of transferring bishops from one diocese to another became common.

In our time, a certain type of Catholic pines for "the good old days: before the Second Vatican Council when, it is mistakenly thought, the Lord's "organizational plan" for the, his church was faithfully honored and implemented.

But we realize now, in the light of history, that what people had become accustomed to in the 1930s, 1940s and 1950s was not at all a part of the unchanging tradition of the Catholic church."

There is also an American historical precedent for the local election of bishops. John Carroll of Baltimore was elected the first American bishop, albeit by his fellow priests, and confirmed by the Pope.

The Institutional Church should move toward a policy of bishops more effectively communicating the needs and wants of the people to the hierarchy for appropriate action.

Re-orienting the Bishops is an important beginning in addressing the subject of Collegiality, which Paul VI pre-empted from consideration during Vatican II. A second reform, suffering the same fate from the Pope is also required for Collegiality to work. That is our next issue.

The Roman Curia

In *A Church In Search of Itself,* author Robert Blair Kaiser writes:

> "A month before the pope (John Paul II) died, Ratzinger had told the chief of RAI's (the Italian state radio station) Vatican coverage that if he should become pope, he wouldn't attempt to reform the Roman Curia. 'I don't know how', he explained, 'Because it's very complicated machinery. It is very difficult to repair complicated machinery. It requires great confidence, which I do not have'.
>
> In fact, Ratzinger developed huge self-confidence before, during and after the conclave, and quite a bit of political cunning, too. Telling RAI before the conclave that he would make no Curial changes would give him a better chance of winning the votes of some Curial Cardinal Electors; they represented 25% of the conclave, and stood to lose their positions in any administrative shake-up."

It appears to me like the first step in Curia reform should be either making its cardinals ineligible to vote for the Pope or ineligible to be elected as Pope and the latter is probably better. The Curia is the administrative and religious bureaucracy that surrounds the Pope. Nominally, the Curia reports directly to the Pope and is responsible only to him. However, there are many who believe that the reverse is true.

For more than 75% of the history of the Church the Curia did not exist, although the concept first appeared in a document written by Pope Urban II in 1089 The first Congregation was not founded for another 500 years, when Pope Paul III established the Congregation of the Inquisition in 1584. Some might argue whether that was the high point or the low.

The Curia has been increased in size and greatly strengthened over the years, especially during Vatican I. It now consists of fourteen Congregations and several lower level departments and tribunals, each of which is responsible for a specific theological aspect of Institutional Church operations. In 1917 Pope Pius X ordered a reorganization of the Curia which was incorporated into Canon Law. In the sixties, Paul VI, ironically also tinkered with what he referred to as reorganization, but both of these efforts amounted to little more than reshuffling the deck. Collectively, the Curia may qualify as the most opaque organization that has ever been created and that includes the Kremlin.

The individual members of the Congregations are rarely mentioned by name or quoted in the world press; their internal processes and deliberations are not public; and it is probably safe to say that outside the Vatican only Vatican scholars understand the full role, mission or purpose of any of the Congregations. We do not know who sets their priorities or monitors their results, much less what their operating budgets are. We know little except that periodically, they release documents, which apparently all are to embrace and unquestioningly follow.

There is no clear cut way for anyone to provide input to a Congregation of the Curia, nor is there any indication that they are interested in it. Methods for resolving issues through the Curia maze are equally obscure.

It would be interesting to learn if any concept, thought or idea which did not originate inside the Curia has ever been embraced or even tolerated by its members. I cannot imagine the frustration and depression of thoughtful and talented devout Catholic theologians, ethicists and philosophers who are outside the Curia and disagree with Curial thinking. And they are also often flirting with excommunication as well.

The Curia is the closest thing that the Institutional Church has to a Presidential cabinet or a government. It could be argued that since it provides advice and counsel to the Pope, it has even more effect than the Pope on the people in the pews. Yet we know very little about its activities. This system is long overdue for reform with the emphasis on transparency.

Clearly, this reform of the Curia is essential for Collegiality to work, which is why Collegiality was tabled at Vatican II. Benedict XVI may, as he claims to "not have the great confidence for that". However, I will bet that we could find someone who has. Perhaps thousands of them.

The morning after I wrote this piece about the Curia I awoke a little before my usual time and lay there for a bit contemplating how to make a transition to the next subject. I suppose naturally, my mind kept going back to the Curia and the image that always comes to my mind when I do.

I have never been to Vatican City and to my knowledge I have never seen pictures of the actual, physical Curia, if it is indeed one place. That said, I am certain that the offices of the various Congregations, Tribunes and other departments of the Curia are among the best, most comfortable and most completely equipped in the world.

However, whenever I think of the Curia I always imagine a building of ten, twelve or more stories, in the shape of a perfect cube. It is made of rough black stone and is completely windowless. It has just one door and no elevators.

Amused by that image, my curiosity took over and I arose, went into my office and turned on the computer. Opening Google Maps, I typed in "curia offices, Vatican City" and selected "satellite photo". The search produced at least a hundred locations which were not merely nearby restaurants, apartments, tourist attractions or otherwise obviously not official curia offices.

I am now not sure which of these two images of the presence of the Curia is more disturbing.

The Pope should form an outside commission of laymen to propose a complete reform and reorganization of the Curia emphasizing transparency and the needs of the laity instead of its own self-interest.

Collegiality

The importance of this reform has in recent years become far more obvious to me and I suspect other Catholics, critical or not than it was during Vatican II. In those days I guess I naively believed that the participation of the Bishops in dialogue and discussion with the Vatican on issues was all that was required to make the Institutional Church more responsive to the needs of its people.

The past sixty years have shown me the fatal error in that supposition. While the bishops were quite effective with their numerical strength among their peers at Vatican II, they have proven that they are impotent in smaller numbers as evidenced by the U.S. Conference of Catholic Bishops. In addition, they have proven time and again that they are not the representatives of the people to the Pope, but merely the messengers of the Curia to the people.

Clearly, Collegiality must include *all* Catholics and the communications structure to make that work must be developed. The issue of the diocesan level election of Bishops as representatives of the people and the reform of the Curia so that there is transparency are manifestations of the importance of universal collegiality throughout the Church at all levels.

It is clear that even if begun today, the level of collegiality required would take a long time to develop. However, that is not a reason to delay the process.

The Church should move immediately toward effective and candid collegiality among all of its elements.

Canon Law

Canon Law is another one of those late-comers to the body of Institutional Church governance. According to the Catholic Encyclopedia, it was not until the First Vatican Council in the eighteen sixties that anyone really thought it was necessary to collect and write down a Code of Canon Law, which Pius X directed to be done. The effort took over fifty years with the first publication appeared, in Latin only of course.

Prior to Vatican II John XXIII called for revisions. It only took thirty-five years to do that job and for most Catholics, Canon Law is still a complete mystery.

The basic problem with Canon Law is that it is not based on a Constitution with a Bill of Rights and therefore there is no way to evaluate the viability of any law. Such a Constitution should delineate the objectives of the organization; assign responsibilities for all its functions; describe how Canon Laws can be enacted; and provide assurances that all Canon Laws are consistent with all the provisions of the Constitution.

Since the Catholic Church has no legislative body or process of debate, the Pope is the Chief Executive and also serves as a one man Supreme Court, one assumes that Canon Law is whatever the Pope says it is. In fact, he often amends some provision that no one even knew was faulty. Precedent apparently has no relevance and certainly justice does not.

Here is a small and somewhat personal example of the efficiency of the Canon Law structure and its appellate process. In 2007, St. Mary's Parish in Jamesville, New York was closed down by the Bishop due to the shortage of priests in the Syracuse Diocese.

My personal connection is that St. Mary's Church was built in 1899 by my wife's grandfather. Her mother and father were married and buried from there. Their two daughters were baptized, made their First Communions, were confirmed and married there, one of them to me. Our niece was married there as were our two oldest granddaughters.

When the parish was closed down in July, 2007, its parishioners began a formal appeal of the Bishop's decision. My wife and I have not been involved in any way with that appeal since we have not lived in the parish for more than fifty-five years.

The parish committee expected to hear before July, 2011 whether or not the Congregation of the Curia designated as responsible will hear their appeal. Not rule on it, just agree to hear it. I suspect that they may be waiting until the church is torn down.

Here is a little anecdotal insight. Congregations and other departments of the Curia are called dicasteries. While writing about the Curia earlier in this chapter, in a futile effort to find a viable definition of a dicastery, I came across this gem:

> *"Since the Supreme Pontiff has immediate, ordinary jurisdiction in every particular church (diocese) in the world, Canon Law affords every Catholic the right of appeal to the Pope.*

This is done through the Roman dicasteries (Congregations, Councils etc.). Letters should be brief, factual and respectful."

Good luck with that.

The Pope should call for an Ecumenical Constitutional Council to draft a formal Constitution for the Church, within which Canon Law can be properly reformed to reflect the world in which we live.

Sexual Abuse By Clergy

This issue is included in the area of governance because it cannot be reduced, much less eliminated except by strong sanctions, constant vigilance and zero tolerance. There is no evidence of any of those attributes in the actions of the Institutional Church. Years after the scandal exploded on our conscious-ness there are still new discoveries of abuse and cover-up.

It is obvious that these criminal acts cannot be handled within the Institutional Church. The only solution is for Pastors and Bishops to be compelled under threat of excommunication to immediately notify local law enforcement when any violation is discovered.

There is nothing else to be said about this issue.

Magisterium

The first time I heard the term Magisterium, I asked what it meant and was told that it was the teaching authority of the Church. That seems simple enough. I took that to be a theoretical abstraction with no rele-vant application in actual practice, like the right to bear arms.

Then I learned that it was a specific mission of the Institutional Church to actually teach the members of the Church about Faith, Morals, Governance and Discipline. I found that interesting and a useful concept. It would be a welcome change from those literal rehashed recitations of the Mass readings passed off as homilies; the unexplained pronouncements of new regulations to be observed; and the uninformed attacks on issues like that on health care reform.

I can't wait until this Magisterium thing begins.

Seriously, Magisterium is an opportunity that the Institutional Church is blowing. In the many discussions I had with lifetime Catholics before I began and have had since I have been writing this book it has amazed me that Catholics are so poorly informed. Real Magisterium could change that.

Time could be well spent on the things discussed in this book and I say that without any pride of authorship or sarcasm. However, as we all know good teaching is an interactive process and doing it only in homilies is not going to work. Positions have to be explained and questioned and "because we say so" is not an acceptable answer. A "take it or leave it" attitude is not a proper approach.

The most important contribution a new Magisterium should provide is an accurate and detailed historical context for the Church. The person in the pew needs to understand who we are as Catholics, where we came from and how we arrived at where we are. The Church should study this issue and come up with a more meaningful and effective Magisterium.

Autochthony

This last issue is a concept, which will be discussed in more detail in Chapter Twelve. It is an alternative with precedent for the Governance of the Church.

Essentially Autochthony is a form of self-governance in the Church such as is practiced in the Eastern Rite churches under the Pope. It appears that it might work for a North American Catholic Church, but there would be many compromises to be discussed and the process would be very long. Ironically, the way things are going it may eventually happen whether anyone wants it to or not.

Chapter Ten

Issues of Individual Discipline

It is completely understandable that Cradle Catholics (those born into families of practicing Catholics and brought up by them) might consider Faith, Religion and Life to be one seamless continuum in which they exist. I understand that simplistic point of view, which I shared for many years.

However, for purposes of clarity about what I mean in *this* book, I have made a distinction between the Catholic *Faith* and the Catholic *Church*; between Faith and Morals in the context of *Faith*; and between Governance and Discipline in the context of *Church*. I consider those distinctions to be legitimate.

In the previous chapter, when I wrote about the Catholic *Faith* I meant that body of beliefs summarized in the Nicene Creed, which I, along with all practicing Catholics acknowledge at every Mass. This faith and the included moral teachings which describe its applications, are contained in dogmas and doctrines based on divine revelation and ecclesiastical tradition.

In this chapter and the next we are going to discuss Church Discipline. This discipline includes all of the rules which the *Institutional* Church has *imposed on the laity* to facilitate its governance of them and to provide what it considers to be proper guidance in living a Christ-like life. In other words it is the *Institutional Church's* definition of what it is to be a Catholic.

Confusion arises because traditionally the Church has used Faith and Morals as a *justification* for the rules and regulations that make up Governance and Discipline and frankly often as a threat to coerce compliance. Sometimes that connection *is* appropriate, but in most of the cases which personally bother the average Catholic, those connections are tenuous or contrived.

Moreover, it is often painfully obvious that certain elements of this code of conduct have been carefully designed to protect the status quo and power of the Institutional Church.

An essential element of the Nicene Creed is the statement, "...we believe in one holy catholic and apostolic Church". I think it is interesting that the Creed doesn't specify that one must *belong* to that "one holy, catholic and apostolic Church", but only that one must believe that it *is* "one holy, catholic and apostolic".

Although I don't want to really get into that discussion, it would appear that the Creed says that one could successfully profess the Catholic *Faith,* without belonging to the Catholic *Church* and that is acceptable. After all, not even the Institutional Church can prevent one from believing what one believes. But I digress.

The Catholic *Church,* on the other hand is a group of people who make up an organization which accepts the Catholic *Faith.* In that sense, being a part of the Church may be considered a manifestation of one's Faith. Furthermore, there can be little argument that, at least theoretically, belonging to the Catholic *Church* can make practicing the Catholic *Faith* significantly easier.

For example, Catholic Church membership provides one access to the sacraments, most especially the Eucharist and all the graces flowing from them. It also provides a procedure, by which one who has committed an offense against the faith or contrary to its system of governance and discipline, can seek and receive forgiveness. Moreover, it provides an orderly structure for worship, collectively performing good works and a rewarding social experience.

All things being equal, there are very strong arguments that belonging to the Catholic *Church* is beneficial to those who believe in the Catholic *Faith*. With minor reservations, I believe that.

The rules of Governance and rules of Discipline should be understandable and able to stand on their merits. If the members of the Church feel that the rules are too onerous or unfair and they leave, they forfeit access to the sacraments, the graces which flow from them and the structure which aids them in living their faith. However, leaving does not necessarily affect their faith.

The Church also has the right to discipline its members for misdeeds against their *faith*, such as disobedience of one or more of the Commandments, since acceptance of that faith is a condition of membership. Furthermore though in a different sense, the Church has the right to discipline members for disobedience of Church *rules*, including those which are *not* matters of faith.

The mechanism for remedying all of these offenses is through the sacrament of Reconciliation and the performing of some kind of penance. The Institutional Church also has the right to terminate membership in the Church through a process called Excommunication. However it seems somewhat confusing to me that the remedy for Excommunication is the sacrament of Reconciliation to which the Excommunicated do not have access. Or are they still Catholics in some kind of virtual prison?

All of this can be very confusing for the average Catholic, mostly because the Institutional Church makes little effort to explain the system. Many traditional, compliant Catholics don't believe Governance and Discipline can be separated from Faith and Morals, even though the doctrine of Infallibility clearly makes that distinction. But then, most of those same people believe the Pope has spoken infallibly in far more instances than he has.

They believe that all positions taken by the Institutional Church have the same weight and credibility. They think we must believe or at least accept everything the Institutional Church teaches us; they consider Faith, Morals, Governance, and Discipline all to be immutable. For them, the Institutional Church is the ultimate example of the cliché "It is what it is". Fortunately, they are mistaken.

In his book *The Church: The Evolution of Catholicism*, Richard P. McBrien says the following about Papal Infallibility In Catholic Teaching (the underlining is mine):

"Unlike for the doctrine of papal primacy, there is no explicit basis for the doctrine of infallibility in the New Testament."

Since we are discussing the church founded by Christ, if it is not found in the New Testament, where might one look? So I guess there is none.

A bit later in the same chapter, Father McBrien makes another point (again, the underlining is mine, but the text has not been changed):

"The key words of the Vatican I text placed certain restrictions on the exercise of papal infallibility: 'When the Roman Pontiff speaks *ex cathedra* [Lat., "from the chair"], that is, when...as pastor and teacher of all Christians in virtue of his highest apostolic authority he defines a doctrine of faith and morals, that must be held by the Universal Church, he is empowered, through the divine assistance promised him in blessed Peter, with the infallibility with which the Divine Redeemer willed to endow his Church.'

Thus, (1) he must be speaking formally as earthly head of the Church (*ex cathedra*); (2) he must be speaking on a matter of faith and morals (not governance and discipline); and (3) he must clearly intend to bind the whole Church. Indeed, the revised Code of Canon Law (1983) stipulates that 'no doctrine is understood to be infallibly defined unless it is clearly established as such' (can. 749.3)."

As I said earlier in this book, a Pope has invoked infallibility only twice during the 150 years it has been claimed. Unfortunately however, whether intentionally or not the Institutional Church has made little effort over the years to clarify this confusion.

How many traditional compliant Catholics understand that distinction? They not only refuse to question the Institutional Church's practices, but they also act as if they are not allowed to do the research to find out whether or not they *can* ask about them. That is what this book is all about.

The Missing Link

There is a fundamental element, which would bridge the separation between the Catholic *Faith* and the Catholic *Church*, which does not exist and I believe is a major source of the problems facing the Church today.

The Institutional Church has no Constitution and therefore no clearly defined *Constitutional Authority*. The Institutional Church has 8,000 pages of Canon Law, but no Constitution on which it is based.

Every other organization to which I have ever belonged has had a constitution. When a new nation is established or an existing government is toppled, the first order of business is to write a new constitution. It is not a simple task, but it can be done quickly and is *because without it, you can't logically do anything else!* Usually, governments are given no more than several months to compose one that is acceptable.

Constitutions define the objectives of the organizations. They outline and guarantee the rights of the members. They define responsibilities and duties of the governing structure (Institutional Church). They specify how rules (canon laws) are made and how disputes are handled. They provide a process for testing the validity of those rules against the objectives of the organization. They determine the ways the leader is determined and they decide what the limits of his or her powers are.

The problem is not however, because the Vatican is unfamiliar with the concept of a constitution. In the Vatican Archives I came upon the Vatican City State constitution, which was updated under the direction of John Paul II in 2000, abrogating the previous Constitution promulgated in 1929.

Did you know that? Neither did I. The Vatican City State even has a President and it isn't the Pope, although under the constitution the Pope retains all the power and authority.

Most Vatican documents, whether issued personally by an individual member of the Curia, officially by the head of a Curia Congregation or Department or by the Pope himself are full of mind-numbing references to scripture, tradition or dogma suggesting a causal relationship to every element of Governance and Discipline that often, if not usually, does not exist. As a result, these documents are all caught up in the doctrine of Papal infallibility.

Theologian Charles E. Curran refers to this phenomenon as "creeping infallibilism" and that is an apt description. That reality has led to the dire condition in which the Church finds itself.

I believe the principal cause is the same for Catholics who leave the Church; for Catholics who stay, but do not attend Mass regularly; and for some Catholics who stay, attend Mass but ignore many of the Churches policies and practices. They all believe Church policies and practices are immutable and that change will never happen. They have lost Hope, not Faith.

I believe that most critical Catholics do accept *teachings* claimed to be the *rationale* for these policies and practices. However, they simply do not agree that an adequate connection has been made between the dogma and the policies and practices. Therefore they do not consider the policies to be just and believe they should be changed. And they are often correct.

Probably because their compliant colleagues do not understand that the doctrine of infallibility *does not apply to matters of governance and discipline*, they believe that matters of governance and discipline cannot be changed. Some of them still refuse to eat meat on Fridays and fast from midnight before receiving the Eucharist.

They do not understand that the reason policies and practices related to governance and discipline are *not* changed is principally because the Institutional Church considers change to be an admission of error or weakness, when it is really a demonstration of intelligence and strength. Changes are not made because they are not in the vested best interest of those in power.

The problem is that the Pope and his minions are more concerned with maintaining the status quo than with the survival of the Church. We have seen in an earlier chapter that prior to Vatican I that was not the case. The Church faced adversity forthrightly and changed to deal with the situation, albeit at a snail's pace.

However at Vatican I, rather than "manning up" against the Modernists *on the merits of their arguments*, they chose to play the "I" card and voted the Pope infallible. That worked until the promise of Vatican II. However, that period of enlightenment was soon recanted and things have gone downhill ever since.

I can hear some of my traditional, compliant Catholic friends mumbling out there saying, "See, there you go.

You are saying that we only have to obey the rules, with which we agree!"

I have never said that and I don't believe that is a valid position. What I *am* saying is that too often the Church, in the interest of maintaining absolute control makes arbitrary rules based on incorrect interpretations, assumptions or faulty logic and frequently all three, which are the opinions of men who, like all of us are susceptible to error. I do believe that when it is *abundantly clear that this is has been done* we are <u>not</u> obliged to remain silent.

I think those affected by these arbitrary rules have, through the exercise of their God-given Free Will the right to question those judgments and the Church has the obligation to respond with an adequate explanation and withstand questioning before the rule is made or sustained. "Because we say so!" or the old favorite "It is a mystery" are not acceptable responses in the case of discipline.

That is not to say that when the rules are questioned the intentions of rules are *always* incorrect or that some less stringent common ground cannot be found. It is merely to say that such a dialogue *must* happen if the Church is to survive.

It is safe to say that few if any critical Catholics expect all of these issues will be resolved in exactly the way they say they might prefer. However they believe that all of those topics I will describe in this chapter and the next as well as some I have not listed must be considered and discussed. We critical Catholics also want an open and full debate in which all affected can participate if only through proper representation by their bishops.

We want cogent and convincing arguments provided for whatever solution is offered and if we are not in good conscience able to accept that decision, we reserve the right to use our God-given Free Will to accept or reject it, to suffer the temporary consequences of that action and to defer final judgment to God.

As I approached this chapter and the one before it on Governance, it was necessary to select the topics with which I would deal. In very short order, I made a list of issues on which critical Catholics believe that the Institutional Church owes us a complete and rational answer and probably a change.

The list has changed as I have gone along with some issues being combined with others and some being dropped because they were really more annoyances than issues. I feel confident that the majority of these issues on the final list will resonate with most of the readers. I also expect that after this book is published I will be asked why I did not include some that are important to some readers and which I will have overlooked.

It should be noted that at my age and state in life few if any of these issues affect me or my family personally. Therefore, I believe that I can be considered an honest broker.

Discipline deals with the rules the Institutional Church has seen fit to impose on all of us to maintain control and the status quo, to guide us through our lives, maintain control and the status quo, help us be more Christ-like, and maintain control and the status quo. Did I mention maintain control and the status quo?

It is the nature of rules that usually there is more than one way to accomplish the same objective. In other words, different rules can have the same effect with substantially different side effects although it sometimes appears that the Institutional Church does not seem to give much thought to that.

During the research for this book, I did some poking around into Canon Law just to get a sense of the documents. There was a phrase, quoted here from Canon 1341: "repairing scandal, restoring justice, and reforming the offender", which I found repeated time and again. The passage continues:

> "Canonical penal law seeks the elusive just balance among these three aims. In the not so distant past, the efforts of church authorities tilted too far toward reforming, or at least at what was perceived to be reforming, the offender and gave insufficient weight to the other two aims. Now that the pendulum has swung in the other direction, it is important that concern for repairing scandal and restoring justice not completely displace concern for the reform of the offender altogether. One of the differences between vengeance and justice is that the latter leaves open some hope for the offender's eventual reintegration into the community. (See Paul Ricoeur, Justice and Vengeance," *Reflections on the "The Just,"* 223-231.)"

It seems to me this reversal of the proper order of priorities may be a root cause for the Institutional Church's significant problems. And, although I understand that restoring justice means punishing him or her, but just what does "reform the offender" mean? Is the Inquisition still going on?

It has turned out that these issues are so complex that it is difficult to discuss them all in one chapter. Therefore, I have made another division of them. In this chapter we will cover Issues of Individual Discipline. These are issues which affect members of the Laity as individual persons. In the next chapter, we will cover Issues of Collective Discipline that is those issues which affect the Laity in general.

Latae Sententiae

For a serious Catholic, Excommunication is the Institutional Church's version of capital punishment. While no one can dispute the Institutional Church's right to expel non-conforming members, few would disagree that should *not* be done without due process.

Latae Sententiae is *automatic* excommunication. You do the act, you are gone. Due process has no role. And sadly, many Catholics may think they have been excommunicated, such as those who have been divorced, when they have not. This is a complex situation.

Latae Sententiae is the moral equivalent of a county court judge at the arraignment of an alleged murderer, pulling out a gun and shooting the prisoner dead. However, there seems to be considerable confusion among Catholic experts as to what and how many offenses currently warrant Excommunications by Latae Sententiae and how that can be forgiven.

The Catholic Encyclopedia says this about Excommunication:

"In the preamble of the Constitution "Apostolicæ Sedis", Pius IX stated that during the course of centuries, the number of censures latæ sententiæ had increased inordinately, that some of them were no longer expedient, that many were doubtful, that they occasioned frequent difficulties of conscience, and finally, that a reform was necessary. On this head Pius IX had anticipated the almost unanimous request of the Catholic episcopate presented at the Vatican Council (Colleetio Lacensis, VII, col. 840, 874, etc.). The number of excommunications latæ sententiæ enumerated by the moralists and canonists is really formidable: Ferraris (Prompta Biblioth., s.v. Excommunicatio, art. ii-iv) gives almost 200. The principal ones were destined to protect the Catholic Faith, the ecclesiastical hierarchy and its jurisdiction, and figured in the Bull known as "In C na Domini" read publicly each year in Rome, on Holy Thursday. In time, this document had received various additions (Ferraris, loc. cit., art. ii, the text of Clement XI), and from it the Constitution "Apostolicæ Sedis" derives excommunications specially reserved, with exception of the tenth.

The Constitution of Pius IX...suppresses all censures latæ sententiæ that it does not retain. Now, besides those which it enumerates it retains:

(1) The censures decreed (and not simply mentioned) by the Council of Trent;

(2) The censures of special law, i.e. those in vigour for papal elections, those enforced in religious orders and institutes, in colleges, communities, etc. As to the censures enumerated, they should be interpreted as if pronounced for the first time, and ancient texts should be consulted for them only in so far as such texts have not been modified by the new law.

Thus the excommunications latæ sententiæ enforced today by common law in the Catholic Church proceed from three sources:

(A) Those enumerated in the Constitution "Apostolicæ Sedis";

(B) Those pronounced by the Council of Trent; and

(C) Those introduced subsequently to the Constitution "Apostolicæ Sedis", i.e. later than 12 October, 1869."

However, conservative Father Phil Bloom, who writes regularly in *Catholic Answer* an extremely conservative magazine, has this to say regarding Latae Sententiae offenses:

"The seven offenses which bring automatic excommunication ("*latae sententiae,* so that it is incurred automatically upon the commission of an offence") are spelled out in canon law. Like legal language everywhere, it is a little bit complex. However, apart from procuring or participating in an abortion, the average Catholic is unlikely to commit one of the offenses. They involve the following: using violent force against the pope, committing a sacrilege such as throwing away a consecrated host, absolving a person with whom one has committed a sin against the sixth commandment, consecrating a bishop without a pontifical mandate, directly violating the seal of confession and formal apostasy, heresy or schism."

There is no possible explanation for why the Pope, living in the cocoon of the Vatican surrounded by the Curia is thus protected yet children exposed to sexual abuse by members of the clergy are not. I find that to be an outrage.

Father Bloom also appears to be in disagreement as to how one can have Excommunication lifted in this answer from his blog *Questions About Catholic Faith*:

> "Let me clear up at least one concern. You can confess the sin of abortion to and receive absolution from any priest. The 1983 code of canon law no longer classifies it as a reserved sin, that is, one only the bishop can absolve. Part of the reason is that it has unfortunately become so common. As you have experienced, that fact does not take away from the terrible feeling of aloneness and isolation. Abortion still is one of seven offenses which bring automatic excommunication, but when the priest gives you absolution, the excommunication is lifted and you can return to communion."

So where does that leave Sister Margaret McBride, the Phoenix nun we talked about in Chapter Two who apparently incurred "automatic excommunication ("*latae sententiae*, so that it is incurred automatically upon the commission of an offence")...(for) procuring or participating in an abortion". In other words, at that point the Archbishop didn't even know about it. She went immediately to her Confessor, told him what had happened and was absolved, which lifted the Excommunication.

It seems to me that either the grandstanding Archbishop or the conservative Father Bloom has egg on his cassock. Either way, the Institutional Church has to get its act together on Excommunication along with dozens of other things. In the meantime, as always, those of us in the pews are kept ignorant and compliant.

One more thought before we leave the subject of abortion. Father Bloom said Canon Law prescribes Excommunication for "procuring or participating in an abortion". This would appear to limit to the offenders to the pregnant mother and the person actually, physically performing the abortion and I have no problem with that.

However, this is a very complex and emotional problem about which I will say more in the next chapter. First I want to finish with some other misunderstandings of automatic excommunication and then address some other Individual Discipline issues with which I have problems.

As I said earlier, the Catholic Church has the right to excommunicate members who no longer meet the qualifications for membership. However, I believe that the Church has the responsibility to review and clarify the rules on excommunication. I see no reason other than contrived stagecraft for Excommunication Latae Sententiae. All excommunications should be carefully considered, be protected by due process and consider the rights of the accused. That is what Justice means.

Over the years I have had several friends, often who were Catholic educated who sincerely believe that to be divorced is to be excommunicated. One recently told me, "When I signed those divorce papers, I was excommunicated Latae Sententiae". That, of course is false on its face because the Church forbids re-marriage not divorce, which it does not even recognize.

Others have told me that they have not sought an annulment since if they were to be successful their children would be de-legitimized and their pastors have allowed them to believe that is true. That practice should not continue.

However, this provides a perfect segue to the next issue.

Treatment by the Institutional Church of Divorced Catholics

I consider marriage to be a very special institution, which should not be trivialized. I think that each partner should expend great effort to preserve every marriage. However, the reality is that some marriages should never have happened; others have just naturally deteriorated beyond repair; and occasionally unanticipated factors have rendered a few no longer tenable.

Too often a divorce is accepted as the solution, usually because one of the partners wants to re-marry. The one who suffers the most is the one who wants to remain a Catholic. That scenario is obviously wrong.

The Institutional Church usually offers counseling when requested, but if it is not requested or the effort fails and the couple divorces, often the Institutional Church lets that just happen. I asked a priest why the Institutional Church does not reach out to people after they have been through a divorce. He bristled and insisted that the Institutional Church *does* reach out, but later admitted that "reaching out" in that case often meant merely responding to a request for information.

When I asked if he didn't think that he should be more pro-active, he admitted that he probably should and indicated that he might use that as the topic for a future homily. Well, duh!

Ironically, in recent years I have noticed parishes organizing social events for single, separated and divorced parishioners. However, I have not seen any references to annulment counseling in the probable event that some serious relationships might develop. Seems like a classical "chicken and the egg" conundrum.

During the research for this book I asked pastors, who were in dioceses separated by a thousand miles or more whether they knew of any divorced members of their congregations who did not receive the Eucharist even though they had not remarried. They all said they did.

When I asked whether they had ever counseled any of those people and informed them of their options, none said they did. I find that appalling.

The Institutional Church forbids any of its members to receive any Sacraments, including the Eucharist, who have received a civil divorce and re-married *without receiving an annulment of their first marriage.* However, if they have not married again they have the same access to the sacraments as any other member.

The Institutional Church has always been secretive and less than forthcoming on the subject of annulment. I had always been told that the process was demeaning, highly complex, extremely lengthy, rarely successful and very expensive.

The truth is that it is conducted very sensitively, fairly simple, takes six to nine months and costs about $150. Perhaps this is where the airlines found the idea of charging a fee for handling one's baggage (sorry, I couldn't resist that). One priest told me that "petitions which are carefully and honestly prepared rarely fail".

The Institutional Church should make this information to all parishioners and allay the common charge that "only rich people can get annulments". The alternative is the continuance of the common practices of people either staying away from the Sacraments or just ignoring the rule that they should.

I believe in the sanctity of marriage and that its permanence should be aggressively supported, but that fact is that there always will be bad marriages. I see no need to change the rules for either marriage or annulments. However, the Institutional Church should insist that pastors be pro-active in counseling and making the annulment process readily available to those who would benefit from it. Take the mystery out of it.

Birth Control

The issue of family planning is among the most troublesome for Catholics in terms of the numbers affected, although it has become a silent issue for many. It is true that some Catholics have used the Institutional Church's position on contraception as an excuse for leaving, but it has always been very easy to find an understanding parish priest willing to give a "temporary" dispensation from the rule with little or no insistence on a reason and no limit on "temporary".

Ironically, those who left the Church over this issue may have done so merely because they accidentally asked a priest who was among the minority refusing such requests. They should have shopped around. Talk about the law of unintended consequences!

That said, I think the Institutional Church has the responsibility to its members to articulate a clearer, fairer and practical position on the matter. This *is* an arbitrary Church Law, subject to revision.

Strangely, there is no specific Biblical or Theological basis for banning contraception except perhaps to strictly fulfill the letter of the Scriptural passage "Increase and multiply". Does that mean to the maximum extent possible? Or is merely an extension of the interpretation of the tenet that procreation is the primary purpose for marriage? Each seems to be a stretch.

No doubt early in history the Institutional Church's interest in banning contraception was to assure a steady and abundant supply of "cradle Catholics". Several years ago on a TV talk show, Father Andrew Greeley was asked why the Institutional Church opposed contraception. His answer was that it was simple: years ago, a couple had to produce seven children to replicate themselves with two adults. Nowadays, producing seven children will, more often than not, yield seven adults. He also said that the Institutional Church had a responsibility to change that arbitrary restriction.

The usual response Catholics receive from the Institutional Church after suggesting that a change is necessary is hostile. It would be interesting to know how many marriages have broken up over the pressure applied by the Institutional Church, especially among *compliant* Catholics who are married to non-Catholics.

It is common today for families to require two full-time parent incomes merely to survive in terms of feeding, clothing, sheltering, educating and parenting their children. It is also well established that for those children to succeed in life, their education must include more than just a high school diploma. Moreover, with all of that pressure on parents, conjugal love between them is essential not just to procreate, but to hold their marriages together.

Still opposition to artificial birth control remains entrenched in the minds of an out-of-touch, old and celibate hierarchy, who have never had to deal with such issues and clearly don't understand them. Paul VI took Birth Control off the table at Vatican II. Nearly fifty years later Benedict XVI is willing to let millions of people die of AIDS in underdeveloped African countries rather than remove a ban on condoms, which most people in developed countries have ignored and will continue to do so. Where is the compassion in that? Or its rationality? What *would* Jesus do?

Perhaps I do not understand the fundamental issue.

Is it the objective of the Institutional Church to assure that married couples produce all the children of which they are capable even if they must bring them up in poverty and deprive them of an essential education? Why is an unborn child of *greater* importance to the Church than one of these who are poor and deprived?

I can immediately think of five families who are friends of mine who produced between eight and twelve children and did an extraordinary job of raising and educating them; and I can think of a larger number who made a mess out of just one child. How can one write a rule that addresses that anomaly?

The Institutional Church preaches that abstinence is acceptable for family planning, even if it is practiced indefinitely. Certainly abstinence reflects the same intent as contraception and abstinence is obviously more effective, if not more practical. In other words abstinence is a fully effective means for achieving a perceived, undesirable end and it is allowed. However artificial contraception, a less effective method is prohibited. Does this make sense to *anyone*?

This ambiguity begs the question of the Institutional Church's conviction in the matter. It appears that the planning is not the issue, the method is. If that is so, isn't abstinence really at the same time the ultimate form of contraception and the ultimate denial of the fundamental purpose of marriage?

I believe a *responsible* couple, that is, a couple who wants the number of children they can properly raise and plans their family using the means they find appropriate, is more likely to be fulfilling the fundamental purpose of marriage than the couple, which is determined to never have children and uses the practice of Institutional Church approved methods to make certain. Show me the fallacy in that reasoning, if you can.

I believe that the number of married couples, Catholic or not who don't want any children at all is very small. However, the majority of them want to be responsible on the issue in terms of their ability to feed, clothe, shelter, educate and properly parent the children they produce. In that sense, they are acting far less recklessly than is their Institutional Church.

I believe that the task of writing a fair, equitable and enforceable rule covering birth control is an impossible task. There are just too many factors entering the equation and too many nuances to be considered.

I think that the best we can do is to agree on some general guideline and leave the conformance up to the *informed* consciences of the people involved.

One could simply restate the primary purpose for marriage more accurately, by saying that *responsible* procreation is one of them. Moreover, I also believe in protecting the innocence and safety of vulnerable children with the need for responsibility in all matters related to their food, clothing, shelter, education and parenting.

I would also add to that list of considerations, the mental and physical health of the parents, particularly the mother. One needs to look no further than the reports of troubled mothers drowning and bludgeoning their babies to death for evidence of that.

I think that one can be consistent with that belief and still plan the responsible composition of one's family, even if that means the temporary use of some form of contraception. In other words, the sin is the result of overall intent, not specific actions. And I don't believe that is the end justifying the means.

The stringent rules against artificial birth control must be relaxed and the responsibility for the judgment involved must be placed with the married couple. The decisions as to how to proceed should be the result of the interaction between their informed consciences and their Free Wills. This should be a major priority for the Institutional Church. Certainly there will be abuses, but probably no more than there are now.

An acceptable, though somewhat arcane, alternative position might be that a marriage is not valid if it is, or becomes, the mutual intent of the parties to completely avoid procreation, without good and sufficient reason. I have known for certain, very few people who have made that specific decision. In any case, I believe that is a matter for the individual conscience.

In Vitro Fertilization

This issue is the polar opposite of Birth Control. These people want to have children of their own, but have not been able to do so. Now let me say when I talk about in-vitro fertilization I am only talking about married couples using *his* sperm and *her* eggs and implanting the resultant embryo in *her* uterus. Period.

I am <u>not</u> talking about genetic engineering, surrogate mothers, sperm donor shopping, non-essential sperm banking, cloning, designer babies, stem cell farming or anything else. I am opposed to all such activity.

In-vitro fertilization is a proven method of procreation allowing practicing Catholics, unable to produce children in the conventional manner, to fulfill the Institutional Church's prescribed reason that they accepted the sacrament of Marriage. However, in-vitro fertilization is currently treated with the same level of condemnation as contraception.

The Institutional Church considers the contraception evil because it is the antithesis of procreation being the purpose of marriage. Why is the opposite not good?

This is an expensive choice for people to make and most of them will not make it frivolously, but as the fulfillment of one of the essential purpose of their marriage it passes the morally responsible test with flying colors. Sometimes God lets us help Him a little and we should welcome that, not make it sound evil, just because we are categorically opposed to admitting that we might have been wrong. That would be arrogant and un-Christ-like.

Why, when there are two married potential parents as the donors, who are merely trying to assure the success of the process of procreation through in-vitro fertilization, should they be criticized and censured? How is that a violation of Natural Law?

The Institutional Church needs to examine in-vitro technology and develop a rational and favorable position which serves the faithful. This is a win-win situation.

Stem Cell Research

In the interest of full disclosure, my wife suffers from Alzheimer's Disease, one of those conditions which might be treated with stem cells. However, she is in the late stages of the disease and stem cell treatment is a long way from reality, so there is no chance that it will help her.

It is a fact that the in-vitro fertilization protocol often produces more embryos than are needed to achieve the desired result. That serendipitously presents a spectacular benefit, stem cells for important necessary research which could lead to prevention or cure of a plethora of devastating diseases.

I have a very large moral problem with "embryo farming", but I have no problem with the scientific use of stem cells from unused fertilized embryos for research, as long as it does not involve cloning. It has often been stated by the scientific community that this source would be sufficient to sustain legitimate research.

With regard to stem cell research, the position of the Church is that it should not be done because in doing so the embryo, which is a human life will be destroyed. It is true that the embryo will be destroyed. There is no question that the embryo is alive. But is that human life?

Scientists and Theologians have long debated the point at which human life begins and, no doubt in order to be as conservative as possible and since one cannot logically assert it happens any earlier, Theologians have held that human life begins when the sperm penetrates the ovum. Before it was demonstrated that this event could, in fact, occur in a laboratory, it was difficult to argue otherwise.

Theologians have also long held that the soul is what distinguishes human life from life of any other kind. Most Christians, Jews and Muslims agree with that concept.

However, demonstrating that a fertilized embryo could exist outside the uterus raises questions concerning the juxtaposition of those concepts. No one can deny that there is life in a fertilized embryo, even when it is sitting in a petri dish. The question is whether it is *human* life at that point and therefore has a soul or whether the soul enters later.

Many other questions flow from that consideration, including:

- Does the sperm carry the soul (not as a component part, per se, but as a *distinguishing* agent) and if so, was it formerly resident in the father?
- Does the soul divide if twins develop or, if not, where does the other soul come from?
- Are the biological parents the only participants in the development of a fetus or does God have a defined role?
- Since in natural conception the ratio of fertilized embryos to viable fetuses is enormous, does that mean that in the course of their lives couples lose literally thousands of children, to say nothing of the fate of their souls?

Perhaps we should look at the fertilized embryo for evidence that the life which it obviously has is really, rather than potentially *human* or if that *distinction* occurs later as the result of a separate event, such as the separate infusion of a soul. The only way we can do that is to look at its evident characteristics as it resides in those laboratory petri dishes and attempt to prove a negative. This is an admittedly difficult task.

I am neither a scientist nor a theologian, but I *have* thought about whether life in a Petri dish can be considered human for quite a while and I consider myself a logical person. What follows is the result of that reasoning process, first articulated in my earlier book, *The Compliant, Curious and Critical Catholic.*

Several distinctive characteristics come to mind, which with great certainty we know exist in those fertilized embryos:

- Though living, they will not develop further until they are implanted in the uterus of a woman.
- They can, unlike life which is human, be frozen, remain in that state indefinitely and then be thawed, remaining alive, yet undeveloped further. And then, if implanted they will develop.
- They require no nourishment during that entire process, unlike life which is known to be human.
- If they are used for another purpose, such as stem cell research, they do not develop another person in that host, but merely new complementary cells.

Those are neither common human attributes nor characteristics. Those facts seem to me to be convincing indications that the nature of the life in those fertilized embryos is not yet human, although it obviously must have the potential to become so.

That begs the question of, if the fertilized embryos in the Petri dish do not have *human* life, at what point does the life they do have, become human?

The Theologian might say, "When the soul enters". The Scientist might say, "When some other event occurs, such as the embryo attaching to the uterine wall". I believe they may both be correct. This does not mean that the soul *is* human life, but that it *distinguishes* it, as in the way its scent *distinguishes* a rose.

Let us look further at the fertilized embryo and we observe the following:

- They will not develop further without implantation.
- Implantation dramatically changes their nature, suggesting that their life is now human and developing, as verifiable immediately with ultra sound pictures (one might assume from the infusion of a soul, but that may be another issue).
- No other explanation is available for that dramatic change in its nature.

Ironically, if the notion is accepted that *human* life begins when the fertilized embryo attaches to the uterine wall, another issue is resolved. At that point it is a fetus, a human being and it is a person. To destroy it then, by whatever means, is to abort a *human* life.

Therefore, we have an interesting corollary to the determination that *human* life begins with the infusion of the soul at the time when the embryo attaches to the wall of the uterus. It strengthens the argument of the Institutional Church against abortion because it is far more definitive and demonstrable through ultrasound imaging than the current position, helping to refute the Pro Choice argument about the first trimester.

It could be argued, perhaps, on the basis that it is contrary to Canon Law and therefore, immutable. However, there is precedent for the Institutional Church changing its position in the face of demonstrable scientific facts. After all, the Church also condemned and excommunicated Galileo for saying the earth revolved around the Sun. Of course it took them 400 years to do it.

I have a very good friend, a very devout Catholic and a doctor who believes that *Humani Vitae,* will be the next theory of heliocentrism.

Now, this is the point when someone from one side of an issue or the other, feeling they have lost the real argument, usually raises the specious, disingenuous and intellectually insulting "slippery slope" theory. That tired metaphor went on life support many years ago when the first skier learned how to traverse and the slippery slope became manageable.

However, the skier knows that after his first traverse down the slope he does not have a *path* but a *process*. Skiing a traverse is about maintaining control and making good decisions along the way. Attempting a slippery slope in any other fashion is reckless and often disastrous.

I believe that this analogy is helpful since it allows us to deal with various Biotechnologies on their individual merits. In my opinion, some can be dismissed without further discussion because they are unacceptable concepts under Natural Law. These include human cloning; genetic engineering (except for the prevention of disease); and the conception of a child primarily to provide spare parts for an older sibling.

On the other hand, this changed position moves the "Morning After Pill" from a matter of abortion to one of contraception. That seems more logical construct for the issue.

This is not to suggest that Biotechnological development must be allowed to proceed unfettered or without moral critique and judgment. The Institutional Church rightfully exercises that prerogative.

In reality however, they have little chance of prevailing in the general sense of banning development of new technology. They can only hope to make their moral point by defining participation by Catholics in the immoral applications of technologies as serious sins. The Institutional Church must also realize that will require far more than "because we say so".

Treatment by the Church of Gays & Lesbians

This is one of those issues, which should be simple, but is made overly complex by too much generalization, false extrapolation and plain old-fashioned bigotry. The result is that certain elements of the Church have behaved abominably with regard to gays and lesbians.

Gays and Lesbians, as children of God should be welcomed into the Church. Two gay men or two lesbian women living together, even if they have civil domestic partnerships should not be excluded per se from Church membership. Instead, they should be subject to the same rules as any other Catholics. They must accept the Faith and the rules of the Church.

They should have the same access to the sacraments as everyone else who is qualified including that they must be in the state of grace to receive the Sacraments, which of course is between them and their Confessors.

Two gay men could not enter into a Catholic marriage, not because they are gay, but because they are both men. The same would be true with two lesbian women. They cannot marry because they are both women, not because they are lesbians. However, it seems to me that if they wanted to a gay man could marry a lesbian woman. Why should it be otherwise?

This issue is simple. If they had been Catholic, the Church would have allowed Bonnie and Clyde to marry. Some tougher issues are in the next Chapter.

Chapter Eleven

Issues of Collective Discipline

O ne of the more rewarding aspects of writing a book is that concentrating and thinking creatively often results in suddenly seeing a situation or a concept or an institution in an entirely different way. This can produce delightful surprises. It happened in the last chapter and again when I began this one.

The last chapter was intended to be a discussion of all the Issues of Discipline on the list I had compiled over several months. Halfway through them I realized the chapter was getting much too long. I did some serious editing, but there still remained the danger of the chapter being more than might be absorbed in one sitting, which always is my guideline for chapter length.

The obvious solution was to make two chapters out of the material. So I began to look at the issues from the standpoint of whether they might fall into logical groupings. When I did that I realized there were two general groups, which were essentially different from one another.

The issues of the first group were those which mostly affected fairly well defined sub-sets of the Laity: younger married couples; divorced people who want to remain in the Church; those with incurable diseases; and homosexuals, just wanting to be welcomed. Those issues remained in Chapter Ten, which was renamed "Issues of *Individual* Discipline".

The issues discussed in this chapter affect virtually *all* of the Laity and therefore I have called them "Issues of *Collective* Discipline". During this process I realized that although they obviously are intended as confessional fodder the issues impacting Catholics collectively are more in the form of general policies rather than specific rules and fall into three distinct classes.

The first and most obvious class is composed of strongly held and clearly stated moral positions, which are generally accepted. The issues here are simple and straightforward and so will be our discussion. Since I don't have problems with most of these things, I have included only that of the opposition to abortion as a primary example and something from which we might learn.

On the other hand, many Catholics have far more serious concerns with the issues in the second class, where there is a *lack* of any strong and clear positions by the Institutional Church. These include poverty, greed, immigration, collective bargaining, affordable health care, the environment, capital punishment and unjust war. Most of these issues are perceived as more important by many Catholics than those in which the positions of the Institutional Church are clearly stated.

Ironically, one certainly might argue that these also are the issues with which Jesus would have been far more concerned. One might also question the motivation for keeping the Institutional Church's teaching on them deliberately vague.

Finally, there are the issues in the third class, which are the annoying problems such as Diocesan taxes on parishes; the lack of transparency in many aspects of Institutional Church finances; a broader role for women in the church; and the general lack of knowledge among the Laity about church history.

Let us begin with the most obvious of those strongly held and clear positions, which make up the first classification.

Abortion

I can almost hear the gasp and sense the anxiety: "Glory, be to God, he is going to come out for Freedom of Choice. He thinks abortion is okay".

Let me first deal with the misuse of the term "Freedom of Choice". One of God's greatest gifts to human beings is that of Free Will. That is Freedom of Choice and it is what defines us. We are the only creatures who have it. I embrace and celebrate that gift. However, we all know it can be used for good or evil.

Freedom of Choice is a good thing and not the issue, the consequence of the choice is. We all have Freedom of Choice and it is not limited to abortion. It has nothing to do with law or morals or right and wrong. If abortion were to be outlawed today, all women would be free to choose to violate that law, just as the thousands of people do every day who choose to commit one of the more conventional forms of murder.

Now with regard to my position on abortion, relax. I agree 100% with the Institutional Church's *basic* position on this. As indicated in Chapter Two, I have some areas of disagreement with the way the Church *applies* that basic position but that is not relevant here. My position is and always has been that elective abortion, which is not medically essential, is murder. Therefore I consider it to be a most grievous sin for both the mother and the person performing it. With all due respect for the Supreme Court, Roe v. Wade didn't change that one bit.

Some Catholics and other Christians believe that since abortion is a most grievous sin against God, carrying with it the possibility of eternal damnation, the state should pass a law making it a criminal offense, which if prosecuted would result in incarceration or worse. However, in the United States which separates church matters and state matters, whether something "is a most grievous sin against God, carrying with it the possibility of eternal damnation" is simply not relevant.

The rationale for establishing an action as "a criminal offense, which if prosecuted would result in incarceration or worse" must be that it is the will of the people within the limits of the Constitution.

I think it is safe to say that the likelihood of the passage of such a law in this country at this time is nonexistent and if it were passed, it would be immediately challenged in the courts. The only way to circumvent that would be a Constitutional Amendment and that is even less likely to happen.

Therefore, the Institutional Church's position and sanction of abortion being "a most grievous sin against God, carrying with it the possibility of eternal damnation" is all that can be done and in truth that is stronger than any man-made law. We need to accept that and move on.

With regard Roe v. Wade, the fact is that if it were overturned today it would not significantly affect the total number of abortions committed each year and in the long run it would make little or no difference except for making it slightly less convenient. The decision to allow abortion or not would revert to the states, where it really is now. Some states would consider that an economic windfall.

There has always been abortion and there always will be. There will always be desperate and uninformed women who do not see it as a choice but a necessity. There will always be prostitutes who view it merely as a treatment for a workplace accident.

I have included this discussion here because I believe that the Institutional Church is completely missing an opportunity to effectively deal with this tragedy by mis-applying resources and energy and wasting them on a fruitless aspect of this issue, the overturning of Roe v. Wade. That is completely foolish.

I believe that most abortions occur not because mothers feel they *have* a choice, but because they feel they *do not* have one and that is the tragedy.

The National Right to Life website shows the number of abortions each year since the Roe v. Wade decision in 1973. Abortions peaked at 1.6 million in 1990. However, from 1992 to 2000 the annual number of abortions decreased by 16%, while the population of 15 to 45 year old women grew by 10%.

The reason for the drop is that during that period the Federal government introduced a number of programs designed to help women get through their unexpected pregnancy and to either keep their baby or offer it for adoption. Starting in 2000 when many of those programs were canceled or had their funding severely reduced, the number of abortions began to level off and since 2004 it has hovered around 1.2 million. However, as a result of the programs which survived the total drop from the peak year of 1990 to 2010 was 25%. I will let you figure out the political reasons for that.

If we were willing to work at it and help pregnant mothers, the abortion rate could be brought down dramatically and in direct proportion to the time effort and resources applied, despite Roe v. Wade. Such an effort has proven far more effective than all the marches, prayer vigils, clinic boycotts, bombings and withholdings of the Eucharist from elected officials combined.

It is time for the Institutional Church to stop all those ineffective and useless demonstrations and divert that energy and those resources to the more practical and productive work of solving the problem by caring for those who are causing it and providing them some tangible alternatives.

I am not necessarily suggesting that more Federal programs are needed. In fact, I am suggesting the opposite. A simple redirection of the energy and resources involved in those marches, prayer vigils, clinic boycotts, bombings and re-application large quantities of the usual Catholic "feel-good-busy-work" could make a powerful difference. Why not organize a grassroots Catholic <u>Un</u>planned Parenthood Association led and funded by the Church?

In addition, we should stop asking people running for election for even minor local offices such as city or town councils and school boards to state their positions on abortion, evolution and other religiously motivated issues over which they have absolutely no control. It makes us look silly, but the Catholic Church is not alone in this activity. We have plenty of ignorant and hypocritical company from the pseudo-Evangelical denominations. Instead of rolling up their sleeves and addressing the problem, they seek political capital from pursuing a legal solution that they know probably will never come and wouldn't work if it did.

Abortion is a moral issue as well as a significant political issue and there is very little wrong with that situation. However, the Institutional Church and more specifically the heavy-handed-bluster-with-no-real-punch USCCB does not understand the old saying about cutting off one's nose to spite one's face.

The strategy of withholding or threatening to withhold the Eucharist from a Representative or Senator because he or she has not promised to vote against the will of their constituents is the ultimate in such unwise, metaphoric, nasal self-mutilation. If the elected official gives in to the pressure it will only assure that he or she will not be re-elected. Moreover, that often means that the person who *is* elected in his or her place will have ideas on *other* issues which will be even more damaging to our country. As the saying goes, "Be careful of that for which you wish".

In early 2011, America Magazine carried this short item on their "Signs of the Times" page:

> "Asked why there was so much disunity on the question of pro-choice Catholics receiving Communion, Denver's Archbishop Charles J. Chaput told the audience at the University of Notre Dame on April 8: "The reason...is that there is no unity among the bishops about it." He said, "There is unity among the bishops about abortion always being wrong and that you can't be a Catholic and be in favor of abortion...but there's just an inability among the bishops together to speak clearly on this matter and even to say that it you're Catholic and you're pro-choice, you can't receive holy Communion." There is a fear, he said, that if bishops speak clearly on the issue, they would make it difficult for Catholic politicians to be elected and would disenfranchise the Catholic community. The strategy clearly has failed, he said. "So let's try something different and see if it works. Let's be very, very clear on these matters."

Aside from being a sad commentary on the bishops in general, the statement absolutely defies plain old common sense. If something is undeniably wrong, punishment may be in order but if the people authorized to administer the punishment cannot agree that punishment is appropriate they should not apply it, because it makes them all look stupid.

With all of its other problems, the Church does not need a bunch of Vigilantes in Mitres running around embarrassing us all.

The supposed political issue here is to prevent the use of Federal tax money to in any way fund abortion. The fact is that the passage of the Hyde Amendment in 1976 is about as close as we are ever going to get on that subject.

By law since 1976 the Hyde Amendment must be attached to the annual appropriations bill for the

Department of Health and Human Services to prevent any program under HHS such as Medicaid, from paying for abortion except in the cases of rape, incest, or where the life of the mother is at risk.

Any law to make abortion equal to conventional murder (although I believe it is) would carry too much emotional baggage to get through Congress and then pass the review of the Supreme Court. To think that even the selection of one more conservative Justice will make the difference is wishful thinking.

To entertain the notion of a Constitutional Amendment, which requires a two-thirds vote in *both* Houses of Congress followed by ratification by 75% of the members of the legislatures in thirty-eight of the fifty states is even more fanciful. It is not going to happen, folks. Give it up.

The current legal status of abortion as permissible murder is not going to be changed and those who think it can be are delusional. If abortion is to be minimized in the United States it will not be done by making it completely illegal. It will only be done by offering pregnant women real and more attractive choices to solve their concerns and problems. Every parish should have such a ministry, staffed by knowledgeable, compassionate and effective people.

It is ironic that this situation exists in a country that was founded with a specific, Constitutional ban on collusion between Church and State. During the days of the Holy Roman Empire, the Church and the Emperor had a pretty cozy relationship. The Pope blessed the coronation of the Emperor, giving the Emperor implicit legitimacy. The Emperor then enforced Church Law and in turn was allowed to influence the selection of the Pope. Very tidy. Very cozy.

However, after the French Revolution the concept of the Holy Roman Empire began to fade and ultimately disappeared. During the same general period, democracies began to follow the enlightened lead of the United States by constitutionally separating Church and State.

Despite that specific admonition, the Institutional Church inappropriately sometimes introduces its positions, noble as they might be into the governing process of the country. In other cases, they duck issues on which a position should be taken raising the question as to why that is so.

Senators and Congressmen are being refused communion or at least threatened with it, regardless of their personal beliefs in the matter, just because they have performed their Constitutional obligation by voting the will of their constituents regarding abortion. Recently an obscure Theologian seeking a little press coverage demanded that the Governor of New York be denied the sacraments because he is living with a woman who is not his wife.

To their credit, several American Bishops disagreed with that condemnation, saying that the living arrangement was a personal matter. However, before any of us get too excited by that glimmer of common sense, I must ask: Isn't there something more important, about which the worldwide Institutional Church ought to be concerned, such as making information on annulments more available?

*****

The second class of Issues of Collective Discipline is far more complex. The passive positions or total lack of any position at all by the Institutional Church on these issues do not universally reflect the views of either major political party. Therefore, at least on the surface they do not appear to be in conflict with the separation of Church and State. These issues are the stuff of a relevant Magisterium as I understand it. I am puzzled as to why they are not addressed. It is as if there must be common cause with some group but who that might be is not readily apparent. That in itself is troubling.

Sometimes it appears that by taking no public position the Institutional Church is merely trying to avoid offending certain people on both sides of the political divide, without any consideration of the morality involved. If that is correct, this begs the question of what is the motivation for this behavior.

However, I am sorry to say that I *think* I may have figured out what is behind this phenomenon, although I cannot be certain and it does not seem to directly apply to all issues. I wonder if you will come to the same conclusion by the end of this chapter.

Poverty

It is time for the American part of the Institutional Church to assert creative leadership in four significant ways and to inspire support for this new approach from the ambo every Sunday. Those ways are:

1. Change the objective from "helping the poor", which has the connotation of an endless process to "eradicating the root causes of poverty", which does not. The first is based on handing out food, clothing and shelter. The second is based on education and creating jobs.
2. Sharpen the focus of all programs for the poor, based on the *premise* that charity begins at home and the *promise* that until poverty is eliminated in the United States no *laity* generated charitable funds will leave the country.
3. Inspire and motivate creativity and imagination in poverty programs. The ideas are there and waiting for the challenge. Every parish has creative people who will respond. Every parish needs to identify them.

4. Place the burden of helping the rest of the world on the countries involved where that is possible and leaving the rest to the charity of Vatican funds.

Some will try to remind me that Jesus said the poor will always be with us and I believe that is true. However, there is a vast difference between being poor, which some economists say is not having as much disposable income as others; and living in poverty, which is an inescapable economic prison.

Our current approach is to make all people in a certain economic class equally miserable, based on the funds which are available. Some of those people are living in poverty for reasons other than economic. They may need to be treated medically or psychologically and we need to do that.

Changing the focus means re-allocating funds ordinarily going to other countries. This is not a selfish move, but the concept of triage applied to poverty. Succeed where you can and only fail where there was little or no hope for real success. It is the only way to break the cycle of poverty.

Poverty is the root cause of virtually every social problem. Poverty is dirty and it smells bad and it is surrounded by myths of despair. Yet poverty persists due at least in part because for many people not touched by it every day, it is a boring problem and it cannot be solved. It is something for which we would rather write a check than spend any time thinking about. For some reason, we believe that all the possible ideas have been tried and didn't work out.

Poverty is a zero sum game. There are hundreds of millions of people suffering from it, not enough people really thinking creatively and just so many resources. As a result, the implicit strategy appears to be a combination of trying to make all the unfortunate uniformly miserable; and periodically responding to the wheel that is squeaking louder than the rest.

The need for creativity, imagination and innovation are so obvious as to be cliché. Don't think outside the box, use the box or burn it. Here is an example.

I spent two solid years from January 2008 through December 2009, doing little else other than trying to develop a concept into a program which would help working poor people in Rochester, New York to become homeowners. My concept ended up in the scrap heap of good ideas but along the way some comic or critic said to me, "OK, so you help them buy a house. How are they going to afford to furnish it? Will they eat standing up and sleep on the floor?"

That was way out of the scope of my project, but the words stuck in my head. It happened that I knew someone who made furniture. Ironically he made church furniture like chairs for the altar, altars, ambos, etc. In other words he made simple quality furniture, built to last with fairly frequent use.

So I asked my friend this compound question: If I were to make space available in the inner city perhaps in the form of an abandoned Catholic school, in which one could build basic, simple, durable and affordable house furniture, could you figure out how the space would be allocated and what kind of equipment would you need; then could you hire and adequately train unemployed, unskilled, people from the area; could you pay them a living wage; could you scale-up the business for say an additional market of college dorm furniture?

His answer was yes on every aspect. Then I asked what his answer would be if the employees were all owners of the enterprise and their compensation of a living wage were partially funded by profit sharing. He said, "Hell, yes!"

A furniture factory is but one example. How about converting another school into a call center; or how about a hydroponic farm with an attached food co-op to sell the produce at cost locally. Could an abandoned church be remodeled into a safe and secure mini-mall for local businesses like barbers, beauty shops, take-out shops, even theaters? Could another be converted into a full service restaurant and attract people from outside the immediate area?

All of these things have the same common thread. They provide good paying jobs, providing needed services and products. They begin to break the cycle of poverty. They teach the poor how to fish!

They could also provide material for years of homilies easily connected to the life of Christ. In itself that is a reason for doing it. Have you had an even better idea while reading this?

Greed

Here is another rich mine for homilies. However, at least in the churches I visit not a word was spoken throughout our devastating recent brush with another Great Depression, except for vague references to the economy, usually tied to a suggestion that the parish needed money too. Its causes, its impact and the lessons to be learned never broke through from the ambo to compete with the giddiness over minor adjustments to the liturgy, like returning to saying "and with your spirit" and the thrill that there will soon be five different ways to say "Go the Mass is finished". (I wonder if Catholics will develop a way to gamble on which one the celebrant will choose each week.)

Christ threw the money changers and opportunistic merchants out of the temple. We sat back and hoped that our loved ones would still get their bonuses. What is that all about? Why weren't Bernie Madoff, the Enron folks, Lehman Brothers, HealthSouth, WorldCom, Tyco, AIG, Waste Management, Freddie Mac and the like excoriated from the ambo? Too close to home?

Although that disturbing possible reason may come to mind, the fact remains that in most parishes these scandals were not even mentioned during those weekly gatherings of the faithful who still go to Mass. Do the priests not understand economics well enough to have an opinion? Are they afraid that there might be some of the architects of that debacle in the congregation and take offense? Why don't they talk about it for *Christ's* sake, if not ours?

Immigration

The position of the Institutional Church on immigration seems to be to treat it as a poverty problem and stay completely out of the debate on how to fix it. The strange thing about this is that all of the elements to solve the problem are clear. The question has become what should be done first? The answer is all of the below must be done at the same time and with all deliberate speed.

Most people would agree that to solve the problem of immigration four things must happen:

1. The borders have to be secure so that the flow of people in and out of the country can be controlled and those who are not eligible to enter are kept out.
2. We must have a simple and efficient means of determining whether a person is who he or she says they are and that includes their eligibility to enter or be here so that employers may determine who they are permitted to hire and who among those they have already employed they may retain.
3. Employers must review all employees to determine if they are legally employable and report those who are not to the proper governmental agency.

4. People from this group who are found to be of good character and have been regularly employed although living here illegally must be offered the opportunity and *be required* to eventually become citizens or they must leave immediately.

These are not steps in a larger process. Together they *are* the process and they must occur simultaneously. Each has an impact on the sensibilities or the wallet of some political constituency. The problem is that different groups of *citizens* accept one or two of the elements and reject the others due to their own self-interest. Some of those who agree with all of the elements do not believe that all must be done at the same time.

The country has the ability and the technology to do the first two items on the list immediately, but strong sanctions must be brought to bear to enforce the third. The process for accomplishing the fourth must be developed and must include penalties in the form of restitution and length of the process. It must be possible, but not overly easy.

The Institutional Church should be involved by way of the *morality* of the situation, pointing out the need for compromise, but not as an advocate for the preferences of any one faction because that just won't work.

Collective Bargaining

It is incredible that this issue is being seriously debated in the twenty-first century. The Institutional American Church has forgotten its immigrant roots. It has forgotten the fields of Cesar Chavez and the sweatshops. It has forgotten Dorothy Day and *The Catholic Worker.*

There is no question that some labor unions, as many organizations (including the Institutional Church), have not acted responsibly and have sometimes misused their power. That should be remedied. However, labor unions have played a vital role in making the country what it is today.

Now they are under attack as never before in the United States and the Church has a large stake in the outcome. Unfortunately, for the most part the *Institutional* Church remains silent or chooses the wrong spokesperson.

To the credit of the USCCB, which I have criticized in this book and will again before we are finished, it said this about wage fairness in an address on Labor Day in 2010:

> "In too many places across America, workers are not being fully paid for their labor. National reports tell of factory workers whose time begins with the start of the conveyor belt not their arrival; of retail workers who are "clocked out" and then required to restock or take inventory; and wait staff whose employers do not give them their tips.
>
> Some unscrupulous employers ignore weak and inadequate laws that forbid such unfair practices in order to increase the bottom line. Families struggling to make ends meet cannot have wage earners shortchanged on overtime or not get paid for all the hours they work. The dignity of the person is diminished when poor or middle-class people are denied their full wage or just compensation for their hard work. A good job at good wages for everyone who is willing and able to work should be our national goal and a moral priority."

Most of you will mentally correct the bishops that some of those comments apply to work rules in addition to wages. However, during the effort in Wisconsin, Ohio, New Jersey and elsewhere to limit or eliminate the time honored right to bargain collectively on such issues there was silence from the ambo. Why was that?

In my opinion, that must indicate that either the parish priests disagree with the USCCB and they should be held accountable for their lack of concern; or the USCCB is trying to have it both ways by being on the record in an obscure statement read by a minority of Catholics and advising their parish priests to not mention it where any laypeople might actually hear it and some might not like it. If the latter is the case, perhaps the priests should consider forming a union.

Now, I feel I must clarify my comment about the USCCB choosing the wrong spokesperson, which certainly damages its moral, if not intellectual credibility.

The message was delivered by a bishop who has been publicly implicated in the cover-up of sexual abuse, including the infamous John Geoghan and Paul Shanley; who was the author of the letter to Congress opposing health care reform (see below); who forbids the distribution of the Eucharist outside the Mass in churches that are unable to have daily Masses, saying that those wanting to receive communion should be directed to churches where Mass is available; who has been accused of evicting a group of elderly nuns and then extensively and expensively remodeling their home as his personal residence; and who, in 2003 during his second year as bishop had to withstand a revolt among his own priests.

While I applaud the USCCB position on collective bargaining, that man does not speak for me.

Affordable Health Care

For most of the debate about Affordable Health Care the Institutional Church remained silent. I found that astounding. There are thirty million uninsured Americans, many millions of whom were victims of the rules on pre-existing conditions and the ability of the insurance companies to cancel policies of people who become seriously ill.

On the face of it, that is wrong. Where was the moral leadership of the Institutional Church on this fundamental issue?

When it looked like the bill might pass, in their questionable wisdom, the USCCB tried to make it an abortion issue, announcing that publicly and calling on their reliable Opus Dei cohorts in Congress to abort the bill. All of the sound moral arguments on the issue were on the side of enacting the bill. The abortion issue was covered by the Hyde Amendment.

However, in my parish the USCCB position was repeated in the homily and printed in the weekly bulletin, prompting an angry e-mail from me to the Pastor. The next Sunday he asked me why I objected and I treated him to the facts. He said he wasn't aware of that.

In the next issue of Newsweek after the USCCB pronouncement the following appeared in an article about the Affordable Health Care bill:

> "This is a major break with the church's bishops, who have strongly opposed the legislation on the grounds that some federal subsidies may end up funding abortions. Although the Senate bill does contain provisions that prohibit the use of federal funds for abortion—similar to the existing Medicaid provisions—bishops have been arguing that the bill is not rigid enough. Nuns disagree.
>
> The nuns who lead 60 different Catholic orders wrote on behalf of their 59,000 members to congressional representatives, saying "despite false claims to the contrary, the Senate bill will not provide taxpayer funding for elective abortion." They call the bill "the real pro-life stance" because it helps pregnant women access the health care they need."

I found it interesting that the day after the Newsweek article appeared, there was an article on a Catholic.org/politics blog attacking the nuns, not so much for their position as for their temerity to express it. One of the comments on the blog said "If *nuns* want to speak out against the *bishops,* it should stay within the Church." *That,* readers is the problem!

However, the USCCB publicly ignored the nuns' statement and so did the pastor and the church bulletin even after I told him about it.

In an article in the New York Times on March 6, 2010 "Does Universal Health Care Discourage Abortions?" writer Catherine Rampell asks the question: Does universal health care reduce the abortion rate? Her reply was:

"T.R. Reid, author of "The Healing of America" (and a former professor of mine), argues:

No one could argue that Germans, Japanese, Brits or Canadians have more respect for life or deeper religious convictions than Americans do. So why do they have fewer abortions?...

The connection was explained to me by a wise and holy man, Cardinal Basil Hume. He was the senior Roman Catholic prelate of England and Wales when I lived in London; as a reporter and a Catholic, I got to know him.

In Britain, only 8 percent of the population is Catholic (compared with 25 percent in the United States). Abortion there is legal. Abortion is free. And yet British women have fewer abortions than Americans do. I asked Cardinal Hume why that is.

The cardinal said that there were several reasons but that one important explanation was Britain's universal health-care system. "If that frightened, unemployed 19-year-old knows that she and her child will have access to medical care whenever it's needed," Hume explained, "she's more likely to carry the baby to term. Isn't it obvious?"

I included this second quote because it supports my earlier point in this chapter on more effective alternatives to reducing abortions.

Presumably, if that were the case it would not have changed the minds of the Bishops, so either they would have prevailed or there would have been no opinion expressed. Good luck with that.

If I didn't know better, I would say that it is possible that the Institutional Church was pandering to the interests of the insurance companies. Come to think of it, I *don't* know better. Have any of you yet detected a common thread here?

The Environment

I would think that if there were one issue on which the Institutional Church would have a strong and unequivocal position, it would be the environment. After all, isn't that the most ubiquitous, most visible gift God has given us?

The April 2011 issue of US Catholic carried the results of two very significant polls on the subject of the environment. The irony of their results is extraordinary.

The first was in an article entitled "Don't Be Crude: It's time to get the petroleum monkey off our backs" by Dan Misleh, Executive Director of the Catholic Coalition on Climate Change. This seems to be a very solid organization and its website is impressive. Its relationship with the USCCB is not clear and a search of USCCB website turned up *nothing* on the environment, but Catholic Coalition on Climate Change website at least carries a rather bland endorsement from the USCCB.

The poll Misleh describes was a survey of 163 visitors to the USCatholic.org website and the results are as follows:

"1. Church leaders should make it clear that it's sinful to have a total lack of concern for how my choices affect the earth and those in poverty.

    72% - Agree

    17% - Disagree

    11% - Other

2. In order to curb my oil addiction, I'm willing to:

    74% - Opt for locally grown and raised foods when grocery shopping.

    68% - Turn down the thermostat in the winter and up in the summer.

    62% - Buy a more fuel-efficient car instead of a gas guzzler when I next buy a car.

    64% - Eat less meat.

    55% - Walk, bike, or take public transportation when possible instead of driving.

    54% - Set my hot water heater to a cooler temperature.

    39% - Take fewer plane trips.

    6% - Get rid of my car altogether.

    22% - Other

    Representative of "other":

    "I try to purchase fewer items in plastic containers and only purchase items in recyclable plastic containers that are recyclable at our city's recycling facility."

3. I think about the consequences that my lifestyle and choices have on the environment:

    45% - Sometimes.

    44% - All the time.

    9% -Not often.

    2% - Never.

4. Most Catholics I know seem to have opinions about the environment shaped more by politicians and pundits like Sarah Palin or Al Gore than by faith.

    60% - Agree

    23% - Disagree

    17% - Other

    Representative of "other":

    "Most Catholics that I know and meet seem to have little or no opinion on these issues."

5. Environmental issues are political issues; they should not be made "religious."

    12% - Agree

    78% - Disagree

    10% - Other

6. Any changes I make in my lifestyle won't really add up to a hill of beans.

    30% - Agree

    55% - Disagree

15% - Other"

It looks like those folks, arguably most likely Catholic have it just about right, but where is the Magisterium on this critical issue?

The other poll was on the "Signs of the Times" page of the same US Catholic issue and it answers that question, which is itself ironic since it was from the *Pew Forum's* 2010 Annual Religion and Public Life Survey. It measured the percentages of U.S. Christians who "Favor tougher environmental laws and regulations" among five categories and the results were:

White Evangelicals	73%
White Mainline Protestants	81%
Black Protestants	79%
White Catholics	86%
Hispanic Catholics	89%

Not bad, but the irony arises from the second result shown, the percentages in each category who say "Religion is the biggest influence on their attitudes about governmental regulations". Not good for anyone, but especially not White Catholics and White Mainline Protestants:

White Evangelicals	11%
White Mainline Protestants	2%
Black Protestants	12%
White Catholics	3%

Hispanic Catholics   9%

While I was writing this I received an e-mail from a close friend on an unrelated matter. In it he said, "We are apparently part of the "Magisterium". How correct he is.

The worst homilist in the world could make an effective argument relating St. Francis to the environment. Where is the creativity and imagination from the ambo? Why are our priests so timid? Why isn't the Institutional Church at the forefront of this debate?

One reason might be that as part of the Restoration (these things really *are* related!) it was decreed that homilies should relate to the Liturgy of the Word. In my opinion, that just points to a lack of imagination or just plain laziness on the part of the clergy. Let's appoint a Cardinal in charge of Homiletic Relevance.

Who says that the only time and place for an Institutional Church position to be made is in the homily, through which many in the congregation sleep? Actions speak louder. Wouldn't an announcement by the Archbishop of New York (the current President of the USCCB) that his Cathedral would be totally green by March 17 of next year in time for the parade be impressive? I wonder why he hasn't done that already. It is a simple concept and dramatically symbolic.

Capital Punishment

A friend of mine once described capital punishment as "retroactive and really late, late-term abortion". I'm not sure that I can do better than that.

Since the discovery of DNA, many capital murder convictions have been reversed. This has led a number of states to ban capital punishment. The Institutional Church should have been in a leadership role in banning capital punishment from the beginning of our republic.

Unjust War

This topic begs the question as to specifically what is Just War. One thing I am positive about is that the second Iraq War was not, but did you ever hear that from the official Institutional Church. Perhaps from some courageous priests, but not from the hierarchy and those priests were probably in trouble.

As a result, more than 4,000 Americans and more than 100,000 Iraqis are dead, but no condemnation by the Institutional Church. There was a mealy-mouthed, cautionary USCCB proclamation on November 13, 2002 before it all began, but it could have been interpreted as saying "if you think you are correct, go for it". However, there has been no condemnation by them of the government not taking proper steps to assure they were indeed correct. If not on this subject, where will we have clear moral, rather than political leadership from our Institutional Church?

*****

Finally we come to the third class of Issues of Collective Discipline, which I call the annoyances because they seem to be saying "these are things we do just because we can and you can just live with it". As such, they symbolize the arrogance of the Institutional Church and the low regard in which they appear to hold those who Vatican II said *are* the Church

Diocesan taxes on parishes

Diocesan taxes are usually called by euphemisms like as the Catholic Ministries Appeal or the Hope Appeal or the Stewardship Appeal or the Catholic Appeal, but since participation in them is not voluntary, they are all really diocesan taxes.

They are taxes rather than legitimate appeals because contributing to them is not optional. There is no risk of shortfall. The bishop determines how many millions of dollars he wants to collect and he allocates "targets" to each of the parishes. They are not targets, they are tax bills. If the parishioners do not donate enough to meet the "target", the pastor must ante up the difference from parish resources. And, to add insult to injury if the "targets" are exceeded, *perhaps*, but not always the bishop will split the surplus. Often he keeps it all.

Certainly the diocese has expenses and certainly the bishop has the right to raise funds for diocesan activities and programs. However, those fundraising efforts should stand on their own merits. A real case should be made by the diocese, supporting the need in detail.

Typically these days, a highly professional video is played in parishes announcing this annual diocesan tax. Attractive and mildly appealing messages are delivered. Unfortunately, there is little detail on such basic things as how much money is to be spent on specific activities, how successful are they and why they are necessary.

It should be that if the bishop makes the case properly, the people agree it is worthwhile and respond, the appeal will be successful. Otherwise, the diocese will have to reduce its plans. That is the way things are supposed to work.

Recently the goal for Rochester Diocese Catholic Ministries Appeal was $5.6 million and because it is really a tax, it was met. There was no alternative.

Render unto the bishop, *what the bishop says is the bishop's!*

Lack of Transparency in Church Finances

Just recently our local newspaper reported that the Diocese had a good year, which was defined as increasing its assets by a bit more than $3 million. No mention of the number of souls saved; the number of homeless sheltered; the adoptions completed; the refugees resettled. No year to year comparisons of baptisms, first communions, confirmations, marriages, annulments, seminarians, ordinations, Mass attendance, etc. In other words, no definition of the way those assets were used.

You see the increase in assets had nothing to do with the operations of the Diocese. Its *investment portfolio* did better this year than last, which screams, not begs, the question: Since the Diocese has an investment portfolio, why doesn't it fund any shortfall in the Annual Appeal?

The point here is that there is no accountability here. Not all funded programs are effective and those which are not should be canceled or modified. Perhaps they are, but who knows.

Sooner or later, closed Diocesan facilities will lose their tax exempt status. What is the plan for that eventuality? Is there one?

The majority of Diocesan funds come from the generosity of the members of the Diocese. Shouldn't they have some accounting of their use?

Isn't that what stewardship means?

And we are not even talking about transparency in the Vatican!

The Role of Women in the Church

Over the years I have heard many men say, "If I were a woman, I would not be a Catholic". I find that a serious indictment of the Institutional Church. I believe that most Catholic men treat the women in their lives with much more respect and courtesy than the Institutional Church does. Despite that, the devotion of women to it is astonishing. However, the anomaly is baffling.

Within the past few months U.S. Catholic magazine reported that 83% of the paid national parish workforce is women, many in high level administrative and managerial positions; that 75% of them have Master's

Degrees and an additional 10% have Doctorates; that one-third of the Catholic students pursuing advanced theological degrees are women and most plan careers in the Institutional Church.

Based on that, it would appear that my premise is totally wrong. Things are really great for women in the Institutional Church. The problem is with that uppity minority who think they should be allowed ordination.

Well, yes that is the problem, but who says they are uppity? However, there are a couple of others and the all reflect the underlying attitude of the Institutional Church toward women.

The same source tells us that the female former seminary student is struggling with the burden of student loans for her education while her classmate, who is the associate pastor had his education paid for. She makes from $20,000 to $29,000 a year during her career, which is a little more than he does, but he doesn't pay much in taxes, lives free at the rectory, drives a parish car and belongs to a country club where he uses the golf clubs a parishioner gave him.

And when he wants to go someplace great on vacation, he can always run a pilgrimage to some holy place with assorted more interesting stops along the way there and on the way back home.

The difference is in attitude toward these women in the workplace and in some cases job frustration. U.S. Catholic reported that "one woman became frustrated when her pastoral counseling sessions had to end with her finding a priest to complete the sacrament of reconciliation. "I walked with these people; I should be able to do this," she remembers thinking."

Others feel threatened when their clerical superiors are changed since they serve at the pleasure of the pastor. At another point the article said "Deacons' wives complete training comparable to or the same as their husbands' only to receive a rose rather than ordination.

A long-time female employee finds herself pushed out to make room for a new employee with a collar—sometimes a deacon with substantially less parish experience."

The average age of these women who keep the Institutional Church operating is 59.5 years. It seems problematic that the next generation of women will tolerate that discrepancy.

One thing wasn't said, but I suspect it is true: Given the option and availability, if the Institutional Church had its choice, except for the most menial tasks, it would prefer to have men in all of those jobs.

That must change.

The Failure of Magisterium in Teaching Catholics About Their Church

One of the most sobering experiences I have had when I began writing this book was that after six years of Sunday School, parochial junior high with the nuns, high school with the Christian Brothers, college with the Jesuits and eighty years of homilies, I suddenly realized how little I really knew about the Catholic Church. The bulk of teaching I had received was limited in scope to less than one hundred years of the first century. It is like repeating the first year of a twenty year education, with a slightly different vocabulary, over and over and over. Or like the movie "Groundhog Day".

I soon found that I was not alone in this ignorance. When I did learn some of the facts here and there and tried to engage friends in discussion of them I was met with blank stares. It is always dangerous to make generalizations. However, although there were a few exceptions my personal observations were that the stronger the convictions were that the positions of the Institutional Church on any of the issues I brought up were totally correct, the less that person knew about the subject. And most of what they did know was anecdotal and hearsay from friends and associates rather than any personal study or research.

Nothing about the Great and not so Great Councils; the East-West Schism; the problems of Luther and Protestantism in general; why Galileo was excommunicated; the morality or lack of same regarding the Crusades; the history of the Papacy. It is as if the period between that covered by the New Testament and today has been sealed in a time capsule and hidden from sight.

It is not that the information cannot be found. The problem is twofold: A lack of intellectual curiosity on the part of the laity; and a systemic failure of Magisterium. Thanks to Google and other search engines one can find literally hundreds of thousands of references, both Catholic and non-Catholic on any subject one wants to explore. No question needs to be left unanswered.

I suspect that the lack of intellectual curiosity is based on the beliefs that such things are not interesting or relevant to their lives and that they cannot change anything anyway. It may well follow that the systemic failure of the Magisterium is actually calculated, based on the realization that if they laity really understood the facts they would demand changes the Institutional Church does not want to make.

The fault in that logic is that the Curia is still living in the Middle Ages when the clergy were the only educated people in the Church. Now they are mostly the less-educated in matters beyond scripture.

In working on this book, while I read material from non-Catholic sources, I constructed my positions and arguments *only* from Catholic sources. One wag, somewhat cynically suggested that I am making the Institutional Church argue with itself. To some extent that is correct. The real Church *is* arguing with itself, every minute of every day.

Yet much was made during Vatican II and the fifty years since about the necessity and importance of meaningful Magisterium.

Great concept. When can we expect it to begin?

Chapter Twelve

(Perhaps) The Ultimate Solution

I suspect that if the Pope called a typical American Catholic's cell phone and asked what he or she would like to have changed in the governance of the Church, the poor parishioner would probably mumble, "Oh, nothing, Holy Father...everything is going just fine. Thank you for asking. Could you send me a Papal Blessing for the family room and perhaps an autographed picture for my office?"

The reality is that not even I would presume to sit down and outline the changes that the Pope *must* make in the organizational structure and governance philosophy in the Church if it is to survive. It is not that I would be particularly intimidated, but he and I are from different cultures and speak entirely different languages regarding the Governance and Discipline.

I suspect that the issues I have raised in this book are not things about which he ever spends much time thinking even though he certainly should. In other words, I really think that if we *did* tell him, he would not "get it" and it would be a complete waste of his time and ours.

Real change in the Institutional Church will *never* come from the top down. There are too many centuries of arrogance, mistrust and vested interests to be overcome. The only way to bring about the changes most American Catholics need and want is from the bottom up. The best for which one can hope is acquiescence by the hierarchy of the inevitable and the recognition that essential change must and will originate in the pews of parish churches all across this country and around the world.

Ironically there is a solution to the problem which at least on the surface seems completely obvious. It is for the Catholic Church in the United States, or perhaps in all of North America to become an autochthonous Church within the Catholic Church umbrella. However, that solution is not without its problems.

It is perhaps not an oversight that *The Catholic Encyclopedia*, published by the *Roman* Catholic Church has no entry for autochthonous although it is fundamental to the universal church. In fact, a search of the entire Catholic Encyclopedia website came up with no referenced use of the word. The concept of American Church autochthony is not within the current collective consciousness of the Vatican.

Autochthonous is generally defined, (initially in Biology) as "Originating where found; indigenous" according to The American Heritage® Dictionary of the English Language, published by Houghton Mifflin Company.

In his Keynote Address on April 19, 2010 to The Humbert Summer School at The Harlequin Hotel, Castlebar, County Mayo in Dublin, Ireland entitled *Catholic Church Reform: No More Thrones*, noted American Catholic author Robert Blair Kaiser further explained autochthonous:

"Now autochthonous is a scary, fifteen-Euro Greek word that is hard to pronounce, but easy to understand. All it means is "home-grown" or "local." But it's an important word because in that concept, we have a legitimate, tradition-tested answer to our principal question: how can we have an accountable Church in Ireland, or Scotland, or the United States, how can we be Irish Catholics, or Scottish Catholics, or American Catholics and still find a place under the Catholic umbrella? We will do it by becoming autochthonous that is not in schism, firm in our traditional Catholic faith, but with a new way of governing ourselves."

Now that does *not* mean that someone, or some parish, or for that matter all of us who have disagreements with the governance and discipline of the Church can just declare themselves autochthonous. That would be anarchy, totally counterproductive and very foolish.

Most Catholics do not realize that the Catholic Church (as distinguished from the <u>Roman</u> Catholic Church) is made up of twenty-three autochthonous Churches.

These twenty-three autochthonous Churches are all *Catholic* Churches because they all accept the leadership of the Pope and share the common Nicene Creed, which according to the Catholic Encyclopedia in its current translation is:

"We believe in one God, the Father Almighty, maker of heaven and earth, and of all things visible and invisible. And in one Lord Jesus Christ, the only begotten Son of God, and born of the Father before all ages. God of God, light of light, true God of true God. Begotten not made, consubstantial to the Father, by whom all things were made. Who for us men and for our salvation came down from heaven. And was incarnate of the Holy Ghost and of the Virgin Mary and was made man; was crucified also for us under Pontius Pilate, suffered and was buried; and the third day rose again according to the Scriptures. And ascended into heaven, sits at the right hand of the Father, and shall come again with glory to judge the living and the dead, of whose Kingdom there shall be no end. And in the Holy Ghost, the Lord and Giver of life, who proceeds from the Father and the Son, who together with the Father and the Son is to be adored and glorified, who spoke by the Prophets. And one holy, catholic, and apostolic Church. We confess one baptism for the remission of sins. And we look for the resurrection of the dead and the life of the world to come. Amen."

I would also venture to guess that most *Roman* Catholics do not realize that the Pope really has multiple, though separate roles in the Catholic universe. He is the Bishop of the Diocese of Rome and as a result he also is the head of the autochthonous *Roman* Catholic Church.

Moreover, by an agreement with the Patriarchs of the twenty-two *other* autochthonous Catholic Churches, the Pope is head of the "umbrella" Catholic Church. This is a permanent arrangement.

On the basis of their unqualified acceptance of the Nicene Creed and the authority of the Pope, twenty-three autochthonous Catholic churches have become "in Communion" with the Pope as head of the *Catholic* Church, which also includes the *Roman* Catholic Church (of which the Pope is also the head). The latest one of these churches to become "in Communion" with the Pope did so in 1930. All of the rest were two to three centuries earlier than that.

In other words, the essence of being *Catholic* is in agreeing with the Pope with regard to the Creed and accepting the Pope as the head of the *Catholic Church* while the essence of being <u>*Roman*</u> Catholic is the additional acceptance of the governance and discipline of the Pope under <u>Roman</u> Catholic Canon Law.

The <u>Roman</u> Catholic Church, which includes nearly all countries in Europe, is by far the largest of these autochthonous Catholic Churches. The other twenty-two are the generally quite small Eastern Catholic Churches and in total they represent only about 2% of the world's Catholics.

In agreeing to be "in communion" with the Pope, they were allowed to retain their own language and liturgy and, most important, *self-governance*, which includes allowing a married clergy. It should be noted that some *other* elements of their governance may be *more* onerous than their current <u>Roman</u> Catholic counterparts. For example, their liturgy can be ponderous and may seem almost unintelligible to members of the <u>Roman</u> Catholic Church.

Moreover, by married clergy they mean that married men *can become* priests. It does not mean that unmarried or widowed priests may take wives. In addition, their treatment of women is even less enlightened than that of the Roman Catholic Church.

None of these Eastern Catholic Churches had a presence in the New World during its development and therefore, Catholics in the United States became de facto <u>Roman</u> Catholics. This is also true wherever the <u>Roman</u> Catholic Church sent missionaries, such as Africa and Latin America.

Therefore, there is no precedent, much less procedure for declaring and establishing the American Catholic Church as autochthonous. That does not mean that it could not be done, but it would obviously be far more complicated than it first may have appeared.

The speaker referenced above, Robert Blair Kaiser recently wrote a novel with the admitted main objective of explaining autochthony and how it might be accomplished. The book is *Cardinal Mahony* (yes, *that* Cardinal Mahony) which is a very entertaining read. In it, Kaiser describes Mahony conceiving and leading a coup by the American Bishops, in which they declare the American Catholic Church to be autochthonous.

The major problem I had with that scenario is that we would still end up at least temporarily with the same Bishops, whose individual and collective incompetence is a major part of the problem, which autochthony would not cure, until most of them could be replaced.

If the Institutional <u>Roman</u> Catholic Church continues in its current mode and fashion, I would welcome the notion of an autochthonous American Catholic Church "in communion" with the Pope and the Catholic Church, but self-governed with its own liturgy, a married clergy and other vital reforms in place. In fact, that may be a viable long-term objective. The emphasis is on "long-term".

In *Cardinal Mahony,* Kaiser alludes to groups in the United States that are actively planning for an autochthonous American Catholic Church. I suspect that was somewhat fictional since I did some Internet research and didn't really find any who were doing that specifically.

I did find several groups that indeed are saying and doing things that could be part of the planning for an autochthonous American Catholic Church. However, I was unable to determine whether these are the groups to which Kaiser referred, whether they are working together, what their real motives and objectives might be or in some cases for that matter, whether they are even Catholics.

As might be expected, many of the groups are single issue oriented (married clergy, ordination of women, birth control, etc.). Others are broader in scope and pattern their structure for an ideal Catholic Church in the image and likeness of the United States Constitution. It would have a House of Representatives composed of lay persons and a Senate composed of Bishops. There would be a Supreme Court and a popularly elected Chief Executive Officer.

What is not readily discernable is how to get from here to there and that is the root of the problem. The Vatican is not going to suddenly decide that American autochthony is a great idea and jump on the bandwagon. We could all hope for the intervention of the Holy Spirit, but the folks in the Vatican have been doing things their own way for so long, I question whether they would recognize her if she showed up in a Ferrari in front of St. Peter's.

In addition, there is an extant anomaly which is patently troublesome. Since there is neither precedent nor procedure, frustrating as it might be, the process leading to autochthony would probably have to have at least the acquiescence of the Pope, since otherwise he could declare it to be an attempt at schism, another of his medieval and arcane powers.

Since by definition an American Catholic Church would continue to subscribe to the Creed and be "in communion" with the Pope the question of schism is probably moot, although it might be a long process to demonstrate that.

That leaves us with the irony that the <u>Roman</u> Catholic Church in America must convince the Pope, in his role as head of the <u>Roman</u> Catholic Church worldwide that he should allow them to form an <u>American</u> Catholic Church "in Communion" with him in his role as head of the "umbrella" Catholic Church.

In doing so, as head of the <u>Roman</u> Catholic Church he would lose a significant portion of the major financial support of Americans. The Curia would lose most of its control over the Americans. It also seems possible that the <u>Roman</u> Catholic Church in Europe and elsewhere would demand the same treatment.

What is in it for the Pope? Why would he agree to this? That solution would have to come from the top down. It is unlikely that it ever will. Certainly not in my lifetime.

I just re-read those last five sentences. Is that any way for a Catholic to talk about the Pope? If the Catholic who says that does so because he wants *his* Church to survive, you're damned right it is!

An autochthonous American Catholic Church could certainly be a significant improvement over what we have now, but only if it is really governed *better*. However, as a practical matter, the paranoia based secrecy of the Curia for the past hundred and fifty or so years has not given us any indication of the ways it is actually being governed today. It would be like handing the keys to your brand new Mercedes to your ten year old child.

This could be the proverbial "Be careful of that for which you wish".

Setting up an autochthonous new Church would be a staggering undertaking, beginning with determining who is in charge of doing it. I would not expect much assistance from Rome and frankly I would be highly suspicious of the motives if it were offered.

Perhaps the best approach would be evolutionary rather than revolutionary. I am sure that some reader out there is saying, "That would be a good idea because of the security factor, since the Church doesn't accept evolution". I just want you to know that I already thought of that.

If the evolutionary approach is chosen, that to which we want to evolve should be clearly stated and options to reach that objective should never be closed. An autochthonous American Catholic Church would be a reasonable and acceptable ultimate objective.

Perhaps it could begin with a forty-five year old version of John XXIII and Vatican III, where the Holy Spirit would be welcomed.

Chapter Thirteen

So...Now What?

The one thing about which we can be certain is that the Institutional Church from the Pope on down through the current Bishops will never do *anything* to remedy any of the issues of Governance and Discipline which have been described in this book. If there are ever to be any changes made, they are going to be forced by the people in the pews, using rational, responsible, purposeful and drastic action.

I believe that the vast majority of the problems facing our Church today are the result of systemic failure (and perhaps some corruption) of the Institutional Church. As Rollo was always reminding Miss Twiddle about the Katzenjammer Kids, "They brought it on themselves".

I believe that in this book, many others and I have demonstrated that the Bishops share this guilt. Their failure to represent the feelings and opinions of the people of their Dioceses to the hierarchy; their failure to deal effectively with the sexual abuse scandals; and their failure to exercise meaningful Magisterium all make them both culpable and complicit. Ironically it also makes them extremely vulnerable to an effort by the laity to begin to force reform.

The major cause of this state of affairs is that the bishops are directed by the hierarchy to only "sanctify, teach and govern" their flocks, not to listen to and advocate for them or in fact to lead them. This absurdity must change quickly. If it is not, the downward spiral of the Catholic Church will continue to accelerate.

All of this could be changed with the stroke of a pen by the Pope. Unfortunately, he is not likely to do that unless under extreme duress since he, his office and the Curia are the most significant part of the problem. It must be remembered that the Institutional Church at the present time is both oligarchic and incestuous. The Cardinals of the Church elect the Pope, usually from their own ranks. The Pope in turn selects the Cardinals, from the ranks of the Bishops and he appoints the Bishops usually on the recommendation of the Bishops and Cardinals.

One hundred and twenty of the Cardinals who are under the age of eighty on the day of the Pope's death vote to elect his successor. To be elected one must receive two-thirds, plus one of the votes cast, so 81 if all those eligible vote. Benedict XVI has appointed 40% of the Cardinals currently eligible to vote for the next Pope and that number can only grow.

Moreover, nearly all of the remaining eligible electors were appointed by John Paul II, most of them based on the recommendations of Benedict XVI when he was Cardinal Ratzinger, in charge of the Congregation of the Holy Office. Anyone one who thinks that the election of the next Pope is not rigged just does not understand how things work.

Now that is not a suggestion that the Holy Spirit cannot make a difference, but these men have free will and essentially owe their careers to the current Pontiff. It is as rigged as it can get.

I consider myself to be reasonably rational. I have devoted considerable time and effort in defining, researching, explaining and crafting a hopefully coherent argument that there are many severe problems in an institution I both love and respect. It would not, however be rational for me to do this without along the way developing a theory for an effective remedy. I will present such a theory. However, since such a remedy is almost by definition far beyond my intellectual and physical abilities to carry out alone, it is equally obvious that extensive assistance is required and I can only provide a call to action.

In this chapter I offer that call to action with a strategy, which I believe would begin that reform. It is simple, but will not be easy, although it appears to be viable.

The premise of the strategy is that although the Bishops are a major part of the problem, they might be an even bigger part of at least a partial solution. The steps in the process are as follows:

- Analyze and make adjustments to the concept of a modern Bishop of today's Church.
- Define the process for the *direct election of bishops by the people of the diocese.*
- Demonstrate strong support for the concept *by the rank and file Catholics in the pews.*
- Define and Specify the Duties of a Bishop under this Concept.
- Apply respectful, but aggressive and effective pressure on the Pope to institute the changes.

These steps must be taken with conviction and in a manner that is not subject to question. They are almost the only solution. If successful, *all future Cardinals will be chosen from the Bishops who were elected by the people and within a generation, Popes will be elected by Cardinals who were elected Bishops by the people in the pews.*

The Concept of a Modern Bishop

Nearly everything about bishops begs for change. The qualifications for the office seriously need to be updated. The selection process is cumbersome; it does not consider *any* input from the people, let alone the priests of the Diocese to be served; and once elected bishops often overstay their effectiveness and their competence. Their job description is not clearly stated and therefore they are not focused on the correct things.

The simple path to changing this situation is threefold:

- Make a few significant additions to the qualifications for selection of a Bishop.
- Change the selection process so that Bishops must be elected by the people of the Diocese in which they will serve, from among the ranks of its current pastors for fixed terms of six years, with one re-election permitted. The election would be subject to the approval of the Pope, but disapproval can only be for causes unknown by the electorate before the balloting.
- Provide a list of specific and measurable duties for each bishop, which has been developed and approved by the people of the Diocese.

I searched for the official and current qualifications of candidates for bishop and found that they have not been updated since the Council of Trent in 1563. That might suggest they need it, even if things were doing well.

They are set forth in Canon Law as follows:

"The Council of Trent determined the conditions to be fulfilled by candidates for the episcopate, of which the following are the principal: birth in lawful wedlock, freedom from censure and irregularity or any defect in mind, purity of personal morals, and good reputation. The candidate must also be fully thirty years of age and have been not less than six months in Holy orders. He ought also to have the theological degree of Doctor or at least be a licentiate in theology or canon law or else have the testimony of a public academy or seat of learning (or, if he be a religious, of the highest authority of his order) that he is fit to teach others."

The following significant additions must be made to this list of qualifications:

- Candidates must be pastors in the Diocese in which they will serve as bishop.
- They must have not reached the age of seventy prior to their initial ordination as bishop.
- They must have the equivalent of a Masters in Business Administration with a concentration in Diocesan Management (it is assumed that any number of graduate schools of business operated by Catholic universities could quickly and easily develop such a concentration of study and would welcome the opportunity to do so).
- Their loyalties must be maintained equally to the hierarchy of the Church and the members of their Diocese and in case of a tie the members of the Diocese prevail.
- They must pledge to faithfully represent the will and preferences of the membership of their Dioceses in all Ecumenical Councils, Synods and meetings of the USCCB.

It is also recommended that the archaic and discriminatory requirement of "birth in lawful wedlock" be stricken from the requirements for candidates.

Definition of Direct Election of Bishops by the People of the Diocese

The popular election of *pastors of the diocese* as their bishop by *the members of* those dioceses is critical to the success of this recommendation. In that regard, let me remind you of the earlier quote in Chapter Nine by Father McBrien in which he said that this procedure is not new, but a return to the practice in effect for 95% of the history of the Church.

The reason for this change is clear from the words of that eminent, though fictional Theologian, Professor Henry Hill in the classic show *Music Man*, when he said to his colleagues, "You gotta know the territory, my friends, you gotta know the territory".

The establishment of term limits is important to eliminate the situation of Bishops remaining in place longer than they are effective. However, this change must be fair to all concerned, so the ground rules for the change would be as follows:

- Two candidates meeting the new qualifications for the office of Bishop will be proposed by a Diocesan Selection Committee consisting of the five senior priests in terms of years ordained in the Diocese and six laypersons of the Diocese chosen by lot from those who have volunteered to serve on that committee.
- If he has not reached the age of seventy and has not already served twelve years as bishop, the current bishop will be given the courtesy of choosing the option to run for re-election, in which case the Selection Committee will only select one other candidate.

Under this concept, all 223 American bishops would stand for election six months from the date of the Pope's affirmation of it. To minimize the future trauma of all elections occurring at the same time, a model based on that of the United States Senate would be used.

The current bishops would be ranked by age and in the Dioceses of the 74 oldest the first election would be for a two year term. Thereafter, their elections would be for the full six year terms. In the Dioceses of the next 74 oldest the first election would be for a four year term, followed by full six year terms. In the remaining 75 Dioceses, all elections would be for six year terms.

Candidates will be named by September 30 and the election will be held by October 31. Members of the Diocese will vote during a period of at least a week in the parish where they are registered. Ordination could therefore take place in time for the first Sunday of Advent, the beginning of the new liturgical year.

When a bishop reaches the end of his second term and is at least seventy years of age, he will be made an Auxiliary Bishop and a new bishop will be elected. Auxiliary Bishops would be retired at seventy-five.

However, if the two-term bishop is not yet seventy, he would be eligible to be considered as a candidate for bishop of any *adjacent* Diocese, where they might be familiar with his reputation, for one additional term.

Obtaining and Demonstrating the Strong Support by the Rank and File Catholics

No one, much less the Pope is going to pay any attention to this concept just because I have written it in a book. In fact, a good friend and fellow author has bet me that I will not be able to get ten bishops (fewer than 4.5% of the 223 in the United States) to read this book. He may be right, but I am certainly going to try.

The even bigger challenge may be to demonstrate that there is strong support for popularly elected, home grown bishops who are committed to listen to the people of their Dioceses and advocate for them on the issues he feels he can support. That is not going to be done by the critical Catholics alone. It must be done by *all* Catholics including those who are otherwise compliant and those who are curious, but not yet convinced.

Part of the problem is that I believe that most compliant and curious Catholics are not comfortable about talking with fellow Catholics about these issues; unfortunately many of them are not knowledgeable about many things in this book and are reticent about venturing an opinion.

For these reasons, perhaps the only way to demonstrate strong support for the concept is through a thoroughly professional and well respected public opinion poll, where the respondents have anonymity in their answers. The crafting of the survey is critical and there can be no grounds for mistrust of its results. Obviously, this poll would have to be conducted in all 223 Dioceses.

Although the punster in me would be delighted if the poll were conducted by the *Pew* Research Center, in the past decade Zogby International has also done a number of excellent surveys on Contemporary Catholic Trends. This would seem to make either of them an ideal choice to conduct such a poll and there may be others as well.

It would seem that one or more contemporary Catholic magazines such as America, Commonweal, National Catholic Reporter and U.S. Catholic would be candidates to step up and sponsor such a poll.

Definition and Specification of the Duties of a Bishop under this Concept

I tried to find an official statement of the current specific duties of a bishop, but the closest I could come was the Vatican II *Decree on the Pastoral Office of Bishops in the Church* which says:

> "A diocese is a section of the People of God entrusted to a bishop to be guided by him with the assistance of his clergy so that, loyal to its pastor and formed by him into one community in the Holy Spirit through the Gospel and the Eucharist, it constitutes one particular church in which

the one, holy, catholic and apostolic Church of Christ is truly present and active.

Bishops should be especially concerned about catechetical instruction. Its function is to develop in men a living, explicit and active faith, enlightened by doctrine. It should be very carefully imparted, not only to children and adolescents but also to young people and even to adults. In imparting this instruction the teachers must observe an order and method suited not only to the matter in hand but also to the character, the ability, the age and the life-style of their audience. This instruction should be based on Holy Scripture, tradition, liturgy, and on the teaching authority and life of the church.

It is therefore bishops who are the principal dispensers of the mysteries of God, and it is their function to control, promote and protect the entire liturgical life of the Church entrusted to them. They should therefore see to it that the faithful know and live the paschal mystery more deeply through the Eucharist, forming one closely-knit body, united by the charity of Christ; "devoting themselves to prayer and the ministry of the word". They should aim to make of one mind in prayer all who are entrusted to their care, and to ensure their advancement in grace through the reception of the sacraments, and that they become faithful witnesses to the Lord.

Those associations also should be inaugurated or encouraged which have, either directly or indirectly, a supernatural object such as the attainment of a more perfect life, the preaching of the gospel of Christ to all men, the promotion of Christian doctrine or of public worship, the pursuit of social aims, or the practice of works of piety or charity."

This certainly is not very specific and not very enlightening. A list of specific and measurable duties much be developed in and for each and every diocese. The bishops should develop them for approval, not of the Pope but of the people of the diocese.

Pressure on the Pope to Accept the Concept

This may in fact be the simplest task of the three. It is the power of the Almighty Dollar.

The idea is simple. Each Catholic will limit the contributions of their family to weekly collections, special appeals and drives and all other fundraising activities to *one dollar each* until the Pope authorizes the popular election of home grown bishops meeting the revised qualifications to six year terms with the possibility of one re-election.

No compromises and no exceptions.

The idea would be that on a certain date Catholics would begin to make their weekly contributions *a dollar bill with the word reform written on its face and not in an envelope.* Those who make automatic contributions from their bank accounts would suspend them and make the direct dollar donation in the collection basket. If widespread, the baskets would be overflowing, but the total amount would be much below average.

The impact would be almost immediate and quite dramatic. Many small, rural churches and those in the inner city literally exist from collection to collection. The Bishop and the more affluent parishes would have to be called upon to help and the strain would be great over time.

The same approach would be used with the annual diocesan appeal. *One dollar.* When those missionaries show up with their compelling stories, videos, and requests, they would be treated the same. *One dollar.* They probably won't return.

It might be well for Catholics who participate in this critical effort, to set aside the remainder of their usual contribution. If they do that, when and if the Pope signs the Apostolic Letter authorizing popularly elected, home grown bishops who are committed to listen to the people of their Dioceses and advocate for them on the issues he feels he can support, they *might* consider making a "catch-up donation" in appreciation. *But not one minute before.*

The reform of the Institutional Church is *critical* to the survival of the Church which serves all compliant, curious, critical and coping Catholics. All of these segments of the American Church *must* come together to make this happen.

No compromises, no exceptions and no excuses.

Chapter Fourteen

A Church Worth Saving

I suspect that at least a few readers of this book if they even got this far, have dismissed it as an unwarranted attack on the Church by a fallen away Catholic whose faith was not very strong in the first place. They would be wrong on all counts:

- I am now in my ninth decade as a full-fledged, practicing, regular Mass attending Catholic and I have never for a microsecond considered leaving.
- I would put the strength of my faith up against anyone with regard to the basic tenets of the Church, as set forth in the Nicene Creed.
- I have *not* attacked the Church, which we all know or at least should know is all of the faithful and that of course includes me.
- My criticism has been carefully researched and is directed to what I have called the Institutional Church or the hierarchy. That criticism has been limited to matters of Governance and Discipline, rather than those of Faith and Morals.
- This criticism is *not* unwarranted. It is long overdue and has been made to save the Church, not diminish it.

My parents were devout, hardworking cradle Catholics who were products of the Great Depression. If you didn't have a strong faith during that period, you were in deep trouble. My father was active in several parish activities, a member of the Nocturnal Adoration Society and for more than twenty years served on the Bishop's Committee on Boy Scouting (I wonder if they have renamed that committee since the recent embarrassments). In today's Church he would definitely be a lector, a Eucharistic minister and perhaps even a Deacon.

My mother was a member of the usual, limited women's parish activities and a person who never met a novena or "never-fail" prayer that she didn't love. Those prayers and novenas all seemed to have different numbers of required repetitions and some of them apparently only worked at specified times on certain days or at particular times of the year. When each came due, I always received a phone call from her the day before reminding me to say them. Of course, two days earlier I had received the "official" text and the required number of repetitions in the mail. And then there was the follow-up call to assure I had not forgotten. Subtlety was not her strong suit.

My sister and I grew up and thrived in that environment of gentle regimentation and formulaic piety. We would not have missed the experience for the world and we in turn passed on our versions of it to our children.

I described my formation as a Catholic in an earlier book, *The Compliant, Curious and Critical Catholic*, published by Xlibris in 2005. I was educated by the Sisters of St. Joseph, the Christian Brothers (FSC) and in college and graduate school, the Jesuits. Catholicism has shaped and guided my life.

My faith has made it possible for me to deal with all of the usual problems everyone faces as well as a few which have not been quite so universal. My parish church has been a refuge when I needed it and the Eucharist has been spiritual nourishment for my entire life. Despite my protestations earlier in this book, I *do* suspect that I have been touched by the Holy Spirit and perhaps more *often* than I realize.

We need the Catholic Church. We need it as the touchstone of our spirituality. We need the sustenance of the Eucharist. We need the strength provided by the sacraments. We need it for community with God. We need it for guidance in our lives. We need the structure the Church provides. We need it to help us raise our children and grandchildren. We need it to inform us on moral and theological matters. We need it to help achieve holiness. We need its help to obtain salvation.

The Institutional Church *needs us* for much more than financial support, although it does need us for that. It needs *us* for credibility among faith communities. It needs *us* for a reality check on *our* priorities and concerns. It needs *us* for objectivity. It needs us because we *are* the Church.

However, during most of my adult life I have witnessed the attempt by the Institutional Church to deliberately marginalize good, devout, practicing Catholics who dare to think critically about issues affecting them personally on a day-to-day basis. The Institutional Church has forgotten that as Blessed John XXIII told us at the beginning of Vatican II, *we are the Church*, something the Institutional Church now treats as an inconvenient truth.

Perhaps that is why declaration of John XXIII as a saint has been stalled since 2000, while the architect of the Restoration to pre-Vatican II thinking Benedict XVI has "fast-tracked" John Paul II, who in his later years carried out that plan of Restoration.

This has been a subtle, but pervasive effort rooted in arrogance and an obsession with power, determined to perpetuate a "one size fits all" version of Catholicism.

I don't believe that is what Christ had in mind. The dichotomy between the Institutional Church and that which is described in the Gospels is stunning, yet no one seems to notice that the Pope and the rest of the hierarchy are walking around as if they were in another century.

I believe this has to change. I believe that the American Catholic Church in which I have lived for more than eighty years is worth saving. That is why I wrote this book.

We Catholics need the community of purpose and mutual support and yes, we need the formality, which could be the hallmark of a properly governed Church with genuinely pastoral discipline. Ordinary Catholics need an approach to governance which listens to their problems and offers solutions rather than a "shut up and do as you are told" response.

As I was finishing this book there were demonstrations in the public squares of Egypt, Libya, Bahrain and all across the Middle East, with angry crowds chanting for regime change, a new constitution, new government, more power for the people. I had a sudden thought albeit fleeting; wondering if that could happen in St. Peter's Square.

It will not. But at the election of some future Pope St. Peter's Square might be less than full, then half empty and eventually down to a handful, mostly from the press.

T.S. Eliot combined the titles of two other works, *The Hollow Land* and *The Broken Men* for one of his most famous poems, *The Hollow Men*. We have all heard its chilling final stanza many times. Let us pray that my substitution of *Church* for "world" is not apt:

> *This is the way the Church ends*
> *This is the way the Church ends*

This is the way the Church ends
Not with a bang but a whimper.

For those of us who are listening, the whimper is deafening. We cannot let that be our fate. I have written this book because I sincerely believe that the Catholic Church is worth saving, which is a good deal more than be said for the attitude of its leaders, from the Pope on down.

Recently, a friend albeit one much more compliant than I, told me that God will not *allow* the Church to fail. At first I thought that meant that no matter *what* we do to try to change the way the Church operates, it will come to naught. In other words, we should "shut up and do as you are told" and everything will work out just fine.

I could not reconcile that belief with the reality that the Institutional Church *has already* failed, as evidenced by all the things in this book and the in the opinions of enlightened Catholic observers, historians and theologians throughout the world. It is like an automobile, travelling on a long, very straight road down a mountain with no gas in its tank and therefore no ability to propel itself, stop or turn. It may appear to be operating properly, but inevitably it will either crash or just slow to an embarrassing stop short of its destination, in the middle of nowhere.

However, I then realized that my friend was actually speaking as a member of the Church described by John XXIII, who said *all of the faithful are the Church*, not just the hierarchy. That is certainly a less compliant point of view than I thought.

In that sense I agree that God will not allow the Church to fail. However, the guys in that out-of-gas car *will not help*. Preventing the failure of the Church will require the support and work of many Catholics. It will require majorities of the *compliant* and *curious* in addition to those who are *critical* and *coping.*

It will need the help of Catholics who *care.* All of these people must help us be heard when we demand that the bishops (who we must be allowed to elect) press for the next Pope be a younger man than most; that he not be tainted by any affiliation with the Curia and that he has the courage to dismantle and reorganize that troubled bureaucracy; that he has the wisdom to embrace God's science along with His myths and His truths; and that he has the vision to re-energize us with new ways of doing things. He will need to listen to *all* the faithful and not just those who tell him what he wants to hear.

That is why I wrote this book. I hope it has made you angry enough to do something.

About the Author

Bob Betterton, a "Cradle Catholic" was born in 1930 in Syracuse, NY, grew up in Blessed Sacrament parish and belonged to the parish sponsored Boy Scout Troop 123. He attended public school through sixth grade, supplemented by the usual "released time" Religious Education and Sunday School, taught by the Sisters of St. Joseph. Bob completed Junior High School at Blessed Sacrament under the full time care and teaching of those same nuns. He then attended and was graduated from high school at the all-boys Christian Brothers Academy.

In 1948, Bob entered LeMoyne College, a Jesuit institution which had opened a year earlier in Syracuse, as a member of its second graduating class, majoring in English and Philosophy, with a minor in Social Sciences. At LeMoyne, in addition to meeting future wife Mona McDermott, Bob was Editor of the campus newspaper, *The Dolphin* and founded a literary magazine, *The Salt Well.* He was elected to the national Jesuit Honorary Society, Alpha Sigma Nu.

Following graduation from LeMoyne in 1952, Bob entered graduate school at Fordham University, where he completed study for an MFA in Communication Arts.

Bob was selected for the Navy Officer Candidate School in Newport, RI and commissioned as an Ensign in April 1954. He and Mona were married that June and moved to Washington, DC for three years, where Bob was assigned as a member of the Navy Security Group. Their first two children, Maryellen and Bob II were born at Bethesda Naval Hospital.

After seriously considering a Navy career, the Bettertons returned to the Syracuse area and Bob went to work in manufacturing with General Electric. He also joined the Syracuse based Navy Reserve Security Group Training Detachment as Executive Officer. Mona gave birth to their third child, Jim in 1960.

General Electric quickly promoted Bob to be its youngest General Foreman and the Navy did the same thing, promoting him to Lieutenant Commander and Commanding Officer of the Detachment. He retired at that rank in 1970.

While at GE, Bob studied in their Harvard Business School developed Manufacturing Training Program and later was on its faculty. He also pursued an MBA from Syracuse University on a part-time basis while at GE and later at Xerox. He was awarded that degree in 1968.

Bob left GE in 1963 and joined Xerox in Rochester, NY, where he had several assignments of increasing responsibility, eventually moving to corporate staff, managing Strategy Development. He remained at Xerox until 1978.

At that point, Bob had been involved in a number of community activities, including bringing the LPGA to Rochester for a tournament in 1977, which he chaired for three years. The tournament grew and prospered. It is now in its thirty-sixth year and is the LPGA Championship, one of the Tour's four major events.

Throughout this period, Mona and Bob were active at St. Louis parish in Pittsford, NY. Mona was a Girl Scout leader for the parish Troup, President of the Women's Association and the first woman to serve on the Parish Council. Bob was a Lector and a Eucharistic Minister.

Their three children attended St. Louis School. Maryellen graduated from Mercy High School and Bob and Jim from McQuaid Jesuit. Maryellen and Bob followed their parents to LeMoyne and Jim attended Marist College.

Impressed by the LPGA Tour and its potential, in 1978 Bob left Xerox and formed his own golf event management company, Sports For Business. Over the next twenty-seven years, during which Mona was diagnosed with Alzheimer's Disease, the company managed Tour players; produced numerous official tournaments for the LPGA and PGA Senior Tours; produced well over one hundred corporate entertainment Pro Am outings; and dozens of charity events.

Bob retired from all of this after 9/11 to care for Mona full-time at home until she entered a skilled nursing facility The Friendly Home in 2006, where she remains today. To stay active he returned to what he had really wanted to do since he was a high school student at CBA. He began to write.

Bob published his first book *The Compliant, Curious and Critical Catholic* in 2005. His second, *The Familiar Stranger Who Lives in Our Home*, which dealt with how he and Mona were able to mange her care at home for fourteen years, followed in 2008.

The Bettertons have nine grandchildren and seven great-grandchildren...so far.

At 81, Bob is thinking about his first novel: the story of a young, married Bishop serving in the time following enactment of the changes proposed in this book. If his writing pattern continues, you can look for it in 2014.

CPSIA information can be obtained at www.ICGtesting.com
Printed in the USA
238686LV00002B/1/P